This World of Echoes

Also by Jacquelyn E. Lane

Once In a Blue Moon
(Illustrator - Jacquelyn E. Lane. Author - Julie Leibrich),

The Children of Gaia
(Author & Illustrator)

This
World
of
Echoes

A Divine Guide
to Being Human

Jacquelyn E. Lane

BALBOA.
PRESS

A DIVISION OF HAY HOUSE

First Published 2012 by Tall Pixie Publishing, New Zealand

www.tallpixie.com

Balboa Press books may be ordered through booksellers or by contacting:

Balboa Press
A Division of Hay House
1663 Liberty Drive
Bloomington, IN 47403
www.balboapress.com
1-(877) 407-4847

ISBN: 978-1-4525-0734-7 (sc)
ISBN: 978-0-9876681-4-1 (eBook I)
ISBN: 978-0-9876681-3-4 (eBook II)
ISBN: 978-0-9876681-5-8 (eBook III)

Printed in the United States of America

Balboa Press rev. date: 10/02/2012

For more information about this book or Jacquelyn E. Lane, please go to the website addresses below.

The three books that comprise *This World of Echoes—A Divine Guide to Being Human* trilogy are also available in digital (eBook) format. Please refer to the websites below or to your eBook retailer.

Websites:

www.jacquelynelane.com

www.worldofechoes.com

Contents

CONTENTS

Preface

Readers are often curious about the source of the writings that comprise *This World of Echoes*. I feel it is important not to be seduced by any claims that such writings come from a particular 'master' or other named being, rather they should be appraised on their content. For me, the test of the wisdom they contain is in the universality of its application, irrespective of any claims about its origin and regardless of the personality through which it is given.

Nearly a decade before I recorded this particular collection, I began to write during my regular evening meditation. I placed myself in a column of light that extended directly from my crown to an apparently limitless height above. (The column is a good way to avoid randomly channelling impressions from the astral plane.) I sent my consciousness up that column of light as high as I could reach without strain. I was met by a clear presence, and then by a sense of group, so far away yet so close. Each presence was distinguishable by its unique energy, and exuded wisdom and love of an order unknown in what we normally think of as our 'human' reality. In response to my questions, words appeared on the inky screen of my inner eye in letters of fiery light.

Over the years one presence came to the fore. It was a being I knew at the depths of my soul, yet from years of meditation experience I felt that it was not my soul. He bathed my very being with the velvet indigo of His love and lit my mind with the bright light of His wisdom. Yet it is important to understand that the higher we go in consciousness the greater our experience of Oneness and distinctions between 'me' and 'not me' dissolve.

As my trust in both my source and myself cemented into more regular meetings, the communications were refined into streams of light, and later became simply energetic parcels of wisdom.

Other teachers and the greater devas also came. Whatever the source, I am still the scribe and as such I take full responsibility for the quality of that scribing. My personality, like that of most human beings, still has to learn all the lessons of the wisdom given in these books!

Sensed impulses from the higher spiritual planes must be filtered through our subtle bodies (mental and emotional) and through our brain consciousness. The clarity of those vehicles, our education and meditation experience are all factors in the translation of those impulses into words on a page.

Often what we think is a separate entity is in fact our own soul and we must learn to distinguish the difference. You will find the importance of communication with one's soul elucidated in many different ways in the trilogy that is *This World of Echoes.*

Because the writings were usually in response to specific questions I posed, or requests for information about a particular topic, many things influenced the themes in these books. In the first book, four of the topics were prompted by themes explored by a sculptor friend in a 1994 exhibition that she felt was an expression of her own spiritual journeying. We had inspired each other for many years with our interest in metaphysics, sharing books, knowledge and experiences. My own studies, discussions with other friends of similar interests, my curiosity and the writings themselves all triggered the many other topics in this trilogy, which was written down over three years from 1995 to 1998.

The text often speaks in the first person 'we' or 'us'. This refers to the source conveying the wisdom; it certainly does not refer to me or to any other incarnate *personality*. In the Devas chapter in Book One, 'we' refers to the devas themselves.

Again, it must be remembered that in the higher spiritual planes, the divisions through which we normally interpret our experience do not exist and beings that live in awareness of the Oneness of All speak from their identification with the I AM of Life, that which we call 'God'. This is true too of the greater devas who, though individually recognisable, identify with the collective consciousness of divinity rather than the kind of separate individuality that characterises human thinking.

The use of capital letters, for example, 'I AM,' 'My,' 'Me,' 'Mine' reference a divine principle or attribute of that which we (often loosely) label 'God'. Other words were given to me capitalised. These distinguish between a personality echo and its divine source, reality or quality, e.g. love and Love, stillness and Stillness. Aspects of the 'divine Trinity' are also capitalised, e.g. Goodness, Beauty, Truth or Will/Purpose, Love, Intelligence, an so on.

For those concerned about the use of the masculine pronoun 'He' when referring to divinity, let me assure you that I would once have been similarly outraged at this apparent affront to gender equity. At one time even the 'God' word irritated me as I struggled to balance conventional religious concepts of God with an expanding spiritual experience. Nowadays, 'He' seems natural to me, both energetically and intellectually, as I have come to understand that its use has nothing whatever to do with the gender of the body we inhabit in a particular life or our ideas of what it means to be a 'man' or a 'woman'.

It is used because the aspect of Deity which we know as Will and Purpose we refer to as the Masculine Principle, whereas the Feminine Principle is divine Substance, the aspect of Deity which has *the intelligence to produce as phenomena what Purpose wills to be.*

The same holds true for the esoteric reference to the human kingdom as being essentially 'masculine'. Esoteric tradition has it that the word 'man' comes from the Sanskrit term 'manas' meaning mind, the distinguishing characteristic of the human kingdom, irrespective of our personal gender in any particular lifetime.

Occasional mention of 'the Christ' in the text are not to the *man* Jesus as he proceeded to his own initiation of 'crucifixion' or 'renunciation' in that lifetime, but to the great being, that *overlighted* Jesus, the 'I', the 'Me', the 'Way' that Jesus referenced.

My deepest gratitude goes to those teachers on the inner planes, including my own soul, who have prompted and guided me through more than four decades of enquiry and study, and who, through the gift of these writings introduced me to an infinite source of joy.

My gratitude goes also to the wonderful teachers of metaphysics whose own work has helped prepare me for these books and enabled the climate of receptivity into which they come. I am grateful to the many who have played a part in the journey, and to those who have unfailingly encouraged me to make these writings available to others.

Everybody, in every walk of life has their part to play in lifting humanity to its next evolutionary state of total soul infusion, when we shall all live as *souls* on Earth, listening not to the echoes but to the original song of Oneness behind them. Let *This World of Echoes* serve you as an introduction to the vast and fascinating topic of the One Life insofar as we are capable of understanding that Life, and as a trigger to your own contemplations.

I trust that like me, you will discover deeper and deeper insights with each reading, and thus be assisted in the challenging task of bringing spirit into matter in your daily life.

Jacquelyn E. Lane

The Server's Prayer

Let all my being be open to Thee
Let all the Light of heaven shine through me
Let me find the stillness of Thy gentle energy
T o be with God is a subtle submission

Let me know at once all planes on which I live
Let earth and sea and sky dwell in my body
And the fire of my spirit and the fire of the Earth
Propel the way for me

Let my past, future and present be placed in service of
    Thee
That all who share Thy Life be uplifted through me.

Book I

Division comes from the Undivided
And thus the Self is born
Yet leaves not the unity
To which it craves return.

Introduction

Wisdom is the direct experience of knowledge. Not 'knowledge' of lists of 'facts' such as fascinates the human mind but the internal knowledge or experience of eternal Truth.

The direct experience is what the human seeks in his spiritual searching through his own institutions of religion, his chosen path of ritual, mysticism or the following of a teacher who may or may not be a 'master'.

There is *no* substitute for the direct experience of knowledge, and words about such knowledge are not the knowledge itself. To one from a fluidless planet who has no experience of water, a *description* of its taste is not equivalent to the *experience* of tasting water.

The direct experience of knowledge is a non-solid transitoriness that transcends the everyday reality of human sense experience. The next best thing to this experience is its symbolic representation in pictures, words or sound. When such word pictures retain as much as possible of the feeling or vibration of the experience, they may serve to lift the consciousness of one who is ready and willing to know to a point where one can realise (experience) the Truth which gave rise to the symbols.

To try to further reduce or translate that direct knowledge into the ordinary is to so dilute and distort the conveyance of original revelation as to turn it into something it never was and it becomes a mere repetition, a diatribe of words. Read these words therefore, not with great effort at comprehension but let them spill across your mind and filter gently through your consciousness.

True knowledge will come not in the action of effort but in the instant when effort is suspended. Revelation, when it comes at all, does so in the moment when the way has been left open, when the brain has stopped its weaving, for the fabric spun of analytical pursuits throws a blind across the pathways down which the light of illumination would otherwise have travelled.

Yes, revelation comes, not in the seeking but in the acceptance of the experience, registered not with the brain but with the whole being.

There are many planes of consciousness. The realm you seem to inhabit is just one of them. The wise teacher recognises the level of the student's delusion and attempts by example of reaction to happenings around them to show a way to a different place of being. Whatever 'level' your learning or whatever dedication to your own delusion, you will find in here something to touch you if you will let it, and slowly or quickly, as is your willingness or not, doors will open to you and a universe of new thought welcome you.

But leave your old ideas behind and do not judge God by the interpretations and fabrications of man's past or present limitations placed around that which is too sacred to profane with trifling rules and petty idolatries built to aggrandise the fanciful notion that God can be made somehow into man's image. Turn this idea on its head and understand instead that it is man's idea of man that must expand before he can uly understand he is made in God's image.

The powerful are never self-righteous, they have no need to be. They never use their power to subdue others, knowing these others to be themselves . They take nothing but give everything because in giving is everything received, and always their power is a state of being not of matter! So begin, not with limits placed on God, but look with open heart and love-filled mind on what is offered and priceless pearls will fall into your hands, not in words or rules or creeds but in your private realisations of Truth perceived.

What is written herein is written not of us but of God. What is written is not just for the benefit of us but for the benefit of all.

When you seek, the answers are already there. Truth stands beside you, not far away. heaven is not far off but abounds within and all around you. Seek no answers that are separate from you for nothing *is* that is separate from you. Question all the world says that does not fill you with warmth and wonderment, and leave aside, unregretfully, all that does not nourish the noblest aspects of your soul or that puts a bar between those others in the world and you.

Impose not your acquired wisdom on others but neither let the pressure of the ignorant, even if it calls itself 'authority,' rob your growing sensibility of Truth which stands, regardless of disapproval. The world would not cease to exist in form if all men were blind and so it is with Truth. It does not cease to be, because one or many of mankind has not eyes to perceive it, not eyes with which the body sees, rather inner sight that learns eventually to distinguish the real from the unreal, God's Truth from man's dogma, and perceptual history, superstition and fantasy from the actual flow of God's energy.

Energy comes in many 'forms,' not just that which you have labelled in your scientific laws, and yet the source of all energy is intent, great or small. Because it is intent that makes your world of form, this book is about the quality of intent.

Any world you want is yours. It is thinking makes it so. But such is the power of your thought that wander it without intent and it returns confusion, intend it with hate and a world of hate hits back at you.

It is so hard to grasp these shifting words that declare at once the unchanging Truth of God and the contingent world of men. But God has Laws you see, and one by one, you will discover these. They are not laws of constraint, dictating how and what and when, but Laws of cause, effect and consequence, and Laws of freedom to choose. The Laws of freedom to choose do not free you from the others.

So it is always when comprehending the gifts of God. You seem at times to fall into confusion for the intellect of man seeks order and constraint and wishes to box things up into parcels small enough to comprehend and manage, so he can say 'I know,' and make finite his conclusions on the nature of being. So, he drives himself into a box, constructing rules, not discovering them, trying to control that over which he can have no control and losing the chance of real power which comes of right to all who are conscious that God is within.

Divine Energy

Naught flows but it has the Word of God behind it. Divine energy is the motion we perceive as flowing from God. We call this motion 'Life'. But the motion is an illusion and this illusion the source of your dearest pleasures and greatest pains.

If this paradox, this idea of illusion, causes revolt in your mind or is at present far from your grasp, let it sit, do not try to argue it away for it is your senses which will provide the arguments and they cannot be relied upon as judges of Truth. Truth is immutable, it changes not, as the judgements of your senses do. Two may view a garden and one declare it fair while the other sees an overgrown tangle of weeds! Yet the garden is unchanged by these opposing views of what it is. And so it is with Truth. It does not change because two of you each behold it differently.

The secret in understanding Truth is to be still and let it reveal itself to you, beyond the 'reason' of your senses, and beyond the dogma of words. Instead, learn to allow it to filter lightly through your heart and higher mind until you learn to see not with the eyes, nor the intellect (which loves a complicated game), but with divine reason.

So let us return lightly, to the subject of energy divine, and perhaps you will learn that there is no motion at all, only God. We make no apology for using the word 'God,' but put aside your view if God to you is some man-like figure upon a throne or some occasionally wrathful patriarch demanding allegiance and ruling the affairs of men in the world. We use the word 'God' because it is a word of power, denoting in its fullest sense the source of all being, Life itself. And because that of which we speak is vastly more than the mundane that humans are inclined to label 'life,' we call God also, 'divine'.

Divine. The word raises the human heart and helps remove the blinkers from your eyes so that they look not outward to the world of forms but inward to the source of soul. It is here we ask your eyes be fixed, and looking in, you will find the Truth standing still before your inner sight. You will glimpse the mystery that Truth is still, and yet from it, everything dances. Divine energy splits into a billion expressions of itself as it flows outward on the wings of its thought.

You see these thoughts as other creatures in the world or as species of animal and plant, or as rocks and mountain heights. But if you were to know them as the energies they are, you would hear them as streams of coloured sound, and behind the coloured sound you would feel that which you call divine, that glorious presence in which all things *are*.

If you attend to the right hand side of your crown, you will hear what seems to be the tantalising distant chorus of angels singing. It is angels singing if you like, but more accurately expressed, it is angel sound. It is in fact your own stream of divine energy you are listening to. It is the thought of you which has sprung forth from the divine mind, like a tourist on an elastic cord, travelling the possibilities of being. Here you are, this stream of sound, reaching the outer limits of your travelling out, and like something on an elastic cord, must you not then bounce back again? Yes, because all God's thoughts must return to It, for there is nowhere else to go.

The products of God's thinking seem to you to be so vast and various that you do not see the patterns of energy repeating themselves in greater and smaller rounds. The structure of the atom is mirrored in the structure of the cosmos, the subtle flows of energy in your lighter bodies are mirrored in the subtle bodies of the Earth. The microcosm and the macrocosm must reflect each other, since in Truth, all is One.

When the higher mind of human kind is awakened, it feels the divine source of all that is in the world. Then you learn to distinguish between what man normally perceives, from the *essence* of being behind every creation. You then realise that to blame God for the world, which is simply other men's actions or perceptions, is to so miss the Truth you might as well blame a mountain for deliberately sitting in your way.

You realise then the irrelevance of argument between schools of thought, be they academic or religious, that it makes as much sense as trying to prove to a bumble bee it is aero-dynamically unsound or lecturing a butterfly that its metamorphosis was purely chemical and therefore not a wonderment of Life at all. Science will always strive to come up with a better explanation of what it 'sees'. But its explanations are actually descriptions, not explanations at all, and the pure scientist understands that true science allows man to describe not just the outer but the inner, and when he grasps the Laws governing the inner, divine Life, he can then construct in the outer world a harmony that at present is seldom known.

When a human discovers divine energy he begins on the road to overcome all limitations of the physical world. How can the outer *not* be mastered by its cause, the inner? When you realise the life you breathe is Life itself, not a mixture of elements called air, then your Life does not cease in the absence of air, as the great masters have demonstrated. But do not be seduced by demonstration! These are given by the great only as proof to doubting minds of what can be accomplished. You cannot demonstrate that which you do not understand, except by accident, and then it is not mastery but happy fate. Such accidents usually seduce a person into thinking it is they who have performed miraculously, whereas the masters know it is the divine Life itself *they* are demonstrating.

What seems a jarring, stumbling mess of life is nothing but the obstacles you placed before the flowing Sound of God. The stream of Life flows round each blockage on your path, not recognising their power to impede its progress. Nor must you impede its progress by your imagining the obstacle is real. By not endowing an obstacle with power you can, with Life, flow past it as a river does a rock within its stream.

Should you erect a dam of such boulders, beware! The river of your life will choke and madly break in wild disarray. Upon the banks of reason will your pent and useless energy be rent. When left alone to do its work the energy of God will move through mountain, tree or you. Your only need or part to play is recognition, and in this recognition is the joy of it received.

Divine energy is Love. Love is the nature of God and is therefore inseparable from the creative power that God is. So find divine energy in all things. Let it seep in through your skin as you stand in a forest or by the sea. Watch it as a stream of light as it opens a flower, and hear it as it waves the trees with wind, and in the many pages that follow you will see it expressed as many things, all aspects of the One thing.

Sound & Light

Deep in the depths of cosmic night, Silence holds all the sound there is, a silence more profound than the deepest thoughts of your imagining. As you travel in that silence behind all sight, you will see Him. He is the Stillness, He is the Silence, but His music is constantly playing. He plays for notes the moons and suns, each note a world contained, for nothing but completeness comes from that which is complete. Each note is round, a sphere of life, its tunes already sung.

Reality is the still Silence of pure Light that we call 'God'. Sound springs forth from Silence, from the Stillness of the One but you hear it not, yet it will tell you so directly the thought of God. For God *is* and changes not, but as God 'thinks' the substance that is God appears to move and thus it is that what we call the universe appears to be. God is One and cannot be divided but as God 'thinks' the apparent motion of His thought seems to divide the undivided and silence becomes sound and stillness, breath. The Light that is *still*, in darkness, motions out in waves that move out and back again in reach according to the depth of the breath that sent them forth. This wave motion has the appearance we call manifestation, the bringing into greater and greater physicality, God's thought. At every level of manifestation the Light sings.

The motion of God's breath creates sound from its Stillness and Light from its darkness for God, being all there is, must contain all sound within His Silence and all motion, which is Light, within His Stillness. Thus the Sound and the Light can only echo that which God *is*. Thus even the angel chorus is but an echo of its source in the Stillness of God. Like an arrow from a bow, the echoes are sent forth and like the string of the bow they must all return to the Stillness again.

As the Light waves forth it has both colour and sound, the two sides of its wave that propel its motion. The quality of the song depends on the Light's consciousness of itself. Thus, the more enlightened the consciousness, the more closely will the song echo the purity of its Light source.

Just as the music of the harp comes in waves from its strings, so each of you is a wave extending out from your source and just as a wave must extend first in one direction, then the other (or it is not a wave) so do you, in all aspects of your being, echo back and forth, as a wave, from your source. Your state comes from the balance of your motion back and forth, your sound from the thinking of your being at its source.

Though the harp-string seems to move, at each point in its journey one can look and see it still, thus the source of its sound is still. As is the harp, so are you. The more you allow your 'productions' to come from the still point of rest, the more power they will have. Time is simply a function of the degree of apparent distance of a waveform from its still point at its source.

Just as God is all there is, there is the One Sound of God that contains all the sound there is and the One colour of God that contains all the colour there is. And so it is and must be with all that appear to be parts of God—those greater and smaller waves of the motion of God's 'thinking'. That sound which a thing is, contains all the sounds that it is. The One note that God is, contains all the notes the Piper plays.

From each note the Piper plays a world tumbles forth and each world's note, a song the angels sing. Just as the One Sound of God contains all there is, so the one note of a world contains all the notes of that world's song and they are sung forth from the Stillness to return to the Stillness when their tune is sung.

So, the stars of heaven sing, each an echo of the One Sound and just as each thing on each world contains within its sound all that it is, so it is contained within the One Sound of all that is. Thus can each be known by his sound and each sound be heard within the One Sound, but if you would know what the true sound of something is, you must attend to its source and not its echo.

All sound, therefore all motion, consequently all manifestation, is only an echo. You are caught in the illusion of materiality by paying attention constantly to outer limits of the echo. You have been seduced by an echo. Power increases as consciousness gives its attention to the source of the echo, that is, as consciousness returns to itself, its point of stillness, being. Thrice blessed are those who hear Sound from Stillness come; first of knowledge for sound is knowing, second of memory for sound recalls, third of Love for sound of Silence speaks.

As each sound reverberates out from the One sound the worlds appear to form. This world is one of sound. Look at the flower and hear it sing. Listen to its song and hear its stillness. Hearken to the Piper and you will hear the angels sing.

On each world a myriad creatures sing. They need you not for them to sing but should you pluck their note mid-song you carry its journey for its motion cannot stop until its song is done. So beware Earthlings what notes you swallow for they dance around inside you waiting to be sung.

You are notes the Piper plays; special thoughts sung to span His worlds of song, to dance the tunes of lifetimes long that link the Piper with His songs, lest they forget that in His Silence they are contained.

Night & Day

Ponder on day and night and you will learn much more than a lesson in the mechanics of bodies in space! They are in fact the outer cloaks that hide the mysteries of Life itself, cloaks that in their movement have fascinated mankind since he set his soul to play on Earth and found himself bewitched by their apparent mistress, time. Time is only a measure of change. Without evidence of change man would not imagine such a thing as time, at all.

Day and night, time and change are the inevitable hallmarks of a physical world. They are the end pieces in a succession of master strokes wrought by that which does not move to give the appearance of movement, wrought by that which changes not to appear as change, and to run the gamut of all it can possibly be. Yet while you watch fascinated, at the endless parade of Life's forming, know that you see only a minuscule demonstration of what it can be.

Many analogies and many mythologies have been used over the ages to describe to the seeker how such a mystery can be, but no words will give what only an insightful mind can see. You will find it stated often in these pages, that what we call God, the divine, cannot be divided. It would be obvious therefore, that such divinity express Oneness. But divinity that is Oneness, and therefore all that there is, must also be able to express all the possibility that there is, including two-ness, three-ness, four-ness and however many billions more possibilities it likes while still remaining Oneness!

If such a Oneness looks within itself, at its potential for being, looks in fact at what it is, it might appear (if it were possible to be outside of that Oneness looking in) to be polarising itself into two, but since it is really only One, then each half of its polarised selves must mirror the other, and snap!—duality seems to be born. And once duality is expressed, it can be expressed again, within each half of itself and so on, until with the multiplication of its thought, a myriad dualities can be seen and with such possibilities can God be said to play.

So it dances, seemingly, out of the One; day and night, night and day, hot and cold, high and low, planet and space. But stop there! All these 'things' are just waves in the One thing, so space cannot be empty, just a less dense expression of the One substance that God, in the imagining of all possibility, has seen within itself, and all of this which God manifests, is God itself.

Ah yes! God itself; the day, the night, the sun, moon and stars, the leaves on trees and water in the sea, the stuff of your bodies, the 'you' of you and the 'me' of me.

And what will you do with this knowledge, when it is grasped? Say, 'Ah hah! I see!' and go back straight away to living in your world as if all were separate things? That is the challenge my friend, with the changing of every day into night and night into day. Will you glory in the sunset and the dawn, but still remember who they are and who it is that watches them?

Day and night is all there is for some of you, yet so much more than this is there for those who change their view. Behind the swirling mass of cycles, is the point from which the pendulum of Life swings. The point to which the pendulum is attached swings not, its very stillness enabling the pendulum to carry its steady beat—back-forth, night-day, growth-decay.

It is the complement of a thought or action that renders itself in universal substance and which 'returns' to you, not as is usually supposed, its opposite, which may be an entirely different quality or nature. This seemingly subtle distinction is important to your completer understanding.

Your thought action goes out from you and imprinting itself upon the substance that God provides of itself to enable the performance of what you call creation, must present its complement to you, the impression that it made upon that substance, just as the ripples from the stone you dropped into a pond come back at last to you. They reach the limits of the energy with which you sent them forth and must come back to you, as their wave, collapsing, returns to the source of itself, in this case you.

Thus the impression of a key in a piece of clay does not give you its opposite, a 'non-key,' but a complementary shape, an opportunity opened by the quality of that key. Again and again you must realise that it is the quality of your intent that returns to you the quality of your thought, its attributes in complementary form that must return to you. So it is that to know yourself of God is to return God to you. To wallow in loneliness will return only loneliness to you.

How hard it is for humans to break habits so negative as these, yet how simple, if only they would let go of their view of reality!

What wonderful simplicity made Earth and its greater home, the universe, each thing a part of Whole, a note making in itself a musicality of notes, and like all the substance of God, each thing upon the Earth receives the complement of the note it sings forth. Greater still are the notes you see not, woven from the mighty plan of angels in the Sun, their spawning children planets bursting forth as life, a countless trillion waves and each of these a wave within a wave. That which seems dead to you may live at other planes, its waves of Life singing beyond reach of your sight, their schools and playgrounds for the soul deafness to your ears.

So complicated is the form and so varied the cycle, you are seduced into thinking the cause is complex. It is simple, but stupendous in its simplicity beyond the grasp of your appreciation and you must content yourself at best on this plane with awe for its Mover. Enjoy the movement, let it thrill you to dance with its beat, but fall in Love with that which it is behind the appearance of it.

When you look up at night and see the stars, know it is Him that you see and in the gladness of your heart you will be close and secure in His beingness, enfolded so well by His might that nothing of the false night will assail you, and when you see the sun rise in the day, recognise the warmth of Him in your heart and it will secure you against the tribulations man sets in his way.

To be in this plane you must keep your own day and night, not literally as darkness and light but as balance of activity and its opposite, rest. Rest allows the motion of God to flow back into the place from which it came. It is the mirror of activity without which no activity can be. As man evolves, he discovers there are many ways to rest, and sleep is not amongst the most efficient for the enlightening ones.

All things of a physical nature must rest, it is true, but you do not always recognise what resting is. It is in fact the reversal of an action, thus if you spend a day in muscle tension you must spend a night in muscle relaxing. Whatever reverses the effect of the activity in which you have engaged is rest. This may seem self-evident, but how seldom do you recognise the quality of the activity in which you engage and therefore know what quality of rest requires the antidote!

When planets move, the cloak of time clicks in. Without movement nothing changes and naught requires rest. The planets round the Earth are like its brothers, shepherding, enabling. Think them not as solid balls of matter hung in space but glowing gates of many lights, conduits of energy, not sat in empty space but placed in substance, solid enough, when viewed from far away!

Suns and moons, night and day, they are given you in which to play out your journey but you have thought it all one way! Yet in you too they have a right to play. These glowing balls of waving light have life that is their own, both host and parent to other forms of life that dwell within, or passing by, stay awhile. As host, they receive and pass the universal rays and by the placement of their orb, so transmit these rays to other orbs. Thus it is in dancing grids the light of cosmic rays traverses space to influence the others in its way. So the arts of grand design go forth and little lives of men are swayed.

Though they seem far away, these planet brothers, orbs of light where beings dwell within, they are a tiny step away as atoms are within your skin. Do you think neighbours so great as these have no influence upon their next of kin?

What wondrous beings reside within these orbs of light! Vaster far in power than any tiny mind of man can deem, for how can God be limited in might or majesty and how therefore can there be limits to His expression? It need concern you not, just know that they are there, not to grovel before in Pagan adulation, but to respect and love in joy and much appreciation for their magnificence, and gratify yourself for the part they play in enabling the steps of your dance and the shaping of your way.

Yet you try to play, probing these gardens of space, seeking with tiny toys the heritage of your race. Never will you know the stars if like a babe you crawl around upon the floor! Find the feet of your spirit and learn to stand. Only then will you see the window or the door through which to gaze and truly see the stars once more.

Spheres

The sphere as a symbol of completeness demonstrates in manifest form, the completeness of God. A sphere with part of itself missing is an impossibility, and not in such a case, a sphere. In fact, a sphere cannot form or be held together in form without being complete. Without all aspects of its sphericity it would collapse.

The energy that holds the sphere together must always be equally both outwards and inwards. Thus the sphere teaches us the basic principle of all expression of consciousness. That which is expressing outwards must be equally held by pressure on it from outside in or it does not hold that particular form but becomes another.

Completeness is a universal Law.

The sphere shows us then the fundamental principle of cause and effect. As the energy of the sphere pushes outwards, it must evoke in universal substance the opposite reaction, the absolute complement to the *quality* of its energy—thus is produced the complementary force that holds it in its spheroidal shape. So it is with all movement in the universe and with all levels and qualities of consciousness producing that apparent movement. (Apparent because as you shall see, nothing in truth moves, but only seems to do so.)

Since there is only one thing in existence, which we name 'God,' there can be nothing outside it and therefore all that happens must take place within God. Any movement within God therefore must be equally mirrored by the 'remainder' of that which is God, thus is the energy of consciousness, the product of 'thinking' shaped into various forms that you experience or 'see'. What you 'see' or perceive depends upon your degree of awareness as part of that One wholeness.

We can say then, that all forms are shaped by the *reaction* of universal substance to the expressing form. Actually, an energy does not become a *form* until it is bounded by the reaction of universal substance to it, and universal substance must exactly mirror the quality of the energy expressing itself, just as when pressing a shape into a piece of clay, we must get an exact indented image of the shape or object in the clay.

This simple, fundamental principle of energy gives rise to all that man calls karma, luck or circumstance. Nowhere can an energy exist without its consequence, its indented image, coming into being.

Thus your thoughts, which are themselves energy, make your experience and at any time a change of thought, a change of quality of consciousness can alter the effect coming back to you. So it is that the great Ones you call masters, as they rise in consciousness to heights undreamed of by so-called 'mortal man,' wipe out karma from their souls and bring instead more glory to themselves and to the universe which touches them.

It is no accident that stars and moons and planets all are spherical in shape or that nature moves in circled spirals. In its expression of perfection the universe moves outward from itself, equally, spherically. But it must also move spirally, to express its infinitude of possibility and in so doing must also move forward and it is this spiraling aspect of the apparent movement of God that gives ye 'mortals' the sense or feeling of time.

You see time as linear however, a misinterpretation of the spiral. Better instead, when thinking of time, to remember always that the sphere is central to all movement in the universe, all expression of God, which is what the universe is.

Thus all forms, at bottom, are spheres, coming into or losing their shape. As it comes into being, striving for perfection, the shape of the sphere will be elliptical. When its energy is spent and it is collapsing from existence as a form, it is also elliptical in shape. Between these states, in the perfection of its balance, it is a sphere radiating outwards from its centre that not one part of it be there without the rest, and in its striving to express all that God is, it must progress and change.

Only from your peculiar vantage point do you see limits to the form. You do not see the movement forward in a spiral motion, 'stuck' as you are in a point of limitation, bounded by the senses. It is only on the inner planes, in the higher mind's silent contemplation, that you can but glimpse the simultaneous expression described herein as spherical, spiralling and forward all at once, in what you label 'time'.

Even structures seeming straight are built on spheres for their smallest parts are such as to reflect the perfect form of the universal mind, in each atom whirling, a tiny, perfect sun.

Divine Communication

Illumination is the lifting of consciousness to the knowledge of God *is*. When you put aside doubt and fear you allow that which *is* to be evident. Communication from the divine is nothing more than the revelation of what *is*.

Freedom lies in the ability to see and hear that which seems to be beyond oneself but is not. Take care then that the object of your thought is fixed on God, not on some limitation you have placed upon yourself. The difficulty arises because man dwells constantly on that which he is not. Only when you cease to fear the world around you can you experience the world as it truly is, an ever-changing stream of the consciousness flowing from that which changes not.

Your consciousness is unbounded, like a river that dips into every crevice, exploring every pathway because it's there. Your river has forgotten it is neither bound by banks nor chases into caverns without the force of will to push its flow. Change the will of your desire to know a different world and your river will be freed from Earthly bounds to flow in what you think is heaven, not a place removed and separate but just behind the world of sight.

Divine communication is the Will of God manifesting as light and sound in the life of any that knows itself to be God expressing as that unique aspect of God which it is. That which is not of God is not real but only the illusion of desire of the mind that wishes it to be so. A divine communication never leads falsely. It never purports to direct but only to be, for God moves not but only *is*. What appears to move is only the expression of that beingness. Herein lies the Stillness of God. Only in the Stillness behind what moves therefore will you find what is real and only in Stillness does God speak. His speech therefore is absolute, filtered only by the veils of imagination you place between your Maker and the swirling mass of doubtful currents you see as you.

Hold to no vision when you seek the Word of God. Speak no word except to orient your mind away from movement created by itself, into the place of silence past which your mind cannot know itself. Seek no chore to offer sacrifice to what you think God wants of you, performing as a ritual mindless movements thought by man to seek a pathway to the One. How can movement find what does not move? How can vision find that which does not pose as sight? Sound and sight may praise God but they do not of themselves lead aright.

To transform your daily lives into life of communion with God, discern the false and you will discover what is true. When you look in the mirror you see that which changes. Flesh fades and dies. 'Beauty' withers before your eyes. Look inside and find that which changes not, until that which changes not is seen as the outside. Never look at the front of things but only at what is behind them. What thought did shape them, what desire designed them?

When you lay aside the self you have constructed as a reaction to 'other man' you remove the limits you have placed upon yourself and begin to know that which God is. Play not in the shadows and trammels of what man says is truth and you will rise above all the pools of darkness even learned judges of the world set to snare the young, for young as children you will be when dropping all the dross of thought you call 'reality'.

When your thought begins with the heart which is the *humaneness* of you and aligned with that which is set above, not below it, the mind will follow the direction of heaven not the desire nature of Earth. For remember, your task here is to infuse Earth with Love that you might help to raise it to a higher expression of good. Yet is it not Good that only in Truth *is*?

Yes, surely, as you see the night follow day what you *see* is not Truth but the accumulation of desire nature deposited in Earth. This does not make Earth evil. How can anything of God be so? It simply is the superficial residue of pattern, of energies set in certain motions continuing to flow.

The Buddha brought Earth wisdom, the Christ eternal Love. That which they have done belongs to everyone, for not one part of either does not permeate the rest. When Christ comes 'down' to Earth He never leaves His heaven. His consciousness is God's and that is why His sight is holy. That is why He speaks the Truth and why He says, 'Arise'. Within you not without you is hid the treasure trove of knowing.

Each time you raise your thought to God, each time you love a flower, tree or bird or puddled ground, you change the quality of flow, and raise the likeness of Earth to heaven. It needs so little, often, to turn the tides of energy that swallow up mankind, just a recognition of the Stillness from which a motion flows.

When you hear the angels sing you hear the sound of Light but do not seek the song to give you heaven's might, for heaven is a place of knowing, whose joy bubbles forth in you, demanding to be sung. Yet God is a wonderment no song explains.

Those who pass through heaven's door remain there, knowing in their hearts that place of stillness regardless of the moves they seem to make elsewhere, regardless of the song through which their 'lives' are sung. Right practise leads to Truth but not of itself is Truth, and right thought merely the pathway cut across one's life to help defray the hell of man's imaginings.

A thought may come to you from words which seem divine. They may lift your heart and light your way, but remember, these movements are not stillness, nor is silence found in sound.

Devas

Those who dwell within the Earth, not imprisoned in soil or stone as you might think, but existing in vaporous planes of light, transport across a space between the solid and the real. For real is that which *is* and 'solid' just a name for a special point of view.

Behind the world of solid form is that which moves all particles that you call life and keeps it by gentle song in arrangements you call form—these forces you have called electrical and gravitational, the 'laws' of science, mathematically precise but missing any thought of intelligent direction as if the whole of nature's wondrous meshing were an 'accident of God'. You know nothing of God if you think it capable of accident!

The intelligence of God has many forms, and some no form at all, but its effect is felt and the character of same you'll find, like any intelligence, is want to give itself a name. So name us devas, we who spin upon the air, yet seldom in the sight of man. We hold the thought of all created form, hold the patterns seen by you as flower, bird or tree. For matter is intelligent, and we the children born of that infusion of solidity with mind. And in this great spawning of our lives, over aeons of years this Earth came alive and we have retreated not. We, both children and creators of the Earth, exist as you do in solid 'natural' form and in mind aware, singing our songs and playing Earth's tune.

Only you go around stumbling, seeing us not, we breathers of fire and masters of wind. You reduce us to analysis, like mere machines or hold us in superstitious awe. Whereas if you would know us and feel we are real in that plane of your thought that lifts off the ground, you would dance here beside us, take joy in our song and learn to respect us as the angels we are.

Let us tell you of that time, long ago when God's thought began to create the Earth. And think you all the creating done? Not so! For we evolve, as you, ever lifting higher to the sun of Light that inside every tiny spark of God must glow. So listen now, and we will tell you how it came to be, the story that as children of the Earth you also ought to understand.

See you here this planet, infused with fiery light, a liquid mass of meltedness. Do you think such fire has no purpose of its own? Nay, you cannot understand such creatures as these who can by the very *stillness* of their mind produce such turbulence as this from which the Earth was wrought. For the greater the stillness, the greater the power, and great indeed is the power that holds centred, a planet, a moon and sky full of suns.

From the stillness and control of the creatures of fire, the lands and the seas were wrought. Through such power as this, the thoughts of God could multiply. Those that are born of celestial wind breathed out this thought of the Earth from the inside of God, and that which you call the winds were born. For that which is created creates itself and God is constantly exploring unending ways to be.

Just as you use beams of wood or steel manoeuvred into place for building, so did we use beams of light to form the structures of the Earth. From these grids the business of living can be conducted upon and within the Earth. Our beams of light are like a channel down which energy runs.

It is powered and maintained by the sun and the great minds that dwell therein.

But it is all a dream you know, this creation of the soul. It is no more reality than is the painting the subject that is painted or the music the emotion it expresses. For Reality is *Stillness*, the Silence of eternal being, the Light you say is 'God,' and you have stayed too long in our creation, convincing yourself our painting, Earth is real. So, you are subject to all that seems outside of you, to all we dreamed together, and some of it seems 'good' and 'right' and some of it seems 'evil'. That is only 'evil' which you deem can hurt you. Can in truth, the music turn and attack the conductor or the painting kill the painter? 'Absurd,' you say, and yet will give your life to almost anything outside you, a tiny thing you call a germ and myriad other fears that eat your mind in what I've called your 'poverty'.

When you reclaim your role as painter or musician, you will take your place with us again as co-creators. You will torture yourselves no more with dreams of death and war, but take in joy with every breath and know that breath, eternity.

Together again, we will play the world, our words tumbling forth in harmony and not at war. And you will hear our song again in every breath of wind, and see our light in every flower, in every beast, in bird and fish and tree.

You will, each one choose aright, rediscover that each of you owns a path that pours in light, a trail from what you are to where you now have come. Turn around and see us there beside you, creatures of the playful air, of liquid life, of flame, of stone. We make you, breathe you, servants all of Life. Come dance with us and know we all are One.

Nature Spirits

Wake up! Wake up! Can you not see them? They dance in beds of flowers, cavort in puddles, ride the sunbeams, howl the wind. Live in movement are these creatures, born of nature's energy, disciplined not, but following their natural path. At the same time they both carry the energy and are the energy that brings sparkle to a garden and vibrance to a sea.

The devas create the tunes the nature spirits play. The dancers of the natural world, they identify with the stream of light a deva sends forth, and becoming that stream, move it through the plants and trees.

Each being that creates, produces countless waves of energy, the echo of their thought in the mind of God, each wave itself a being, moving through its world. The same is with your thought, creating ripples through your world. The thoughts assume independence, once released, to play until withdrawn, back into the mind creating them.

So it is with creatures such as these, that when man destroys their habitat by callousness or greed, their life withdraws. For how can it find expression when that in which it resonated—a plant, or forest tree—is gone, or altered such by man to render incompatibility with the grand design of devic intent, and part of God's expression express no more, withdrawn to its source to leave man alone with his consequences. But devas want to sing and nature spirits love to play and when a human welcomes them and open hearted asks to hear their song, the devas rush with glad delight, spilling child-like spirits out upon the world and human beings delight in healthy gardens, sparkling seas and forest glades to heal the heart and spread the fruits of countless trees.

Do not stand apart and see them just as dancing fairy rings, but try to understand these energies weave webs of light that bind with love of being the fabric of the world. They take your share of laughter with them in the world. Love will heal for it is whole, so call them forth wherever Earth, bereft of Life, needs healing. But first prepare the ground with love and healing of your own. Cleanse it free of negativity and hurt of carelessness. Sweep all that fouled a perfect place and send it into Light that knows no loss or imperfection.

Work in groups of ones who Love and when your work of cleansing's done, invite the nature spirits there. Consult their devic counterparts and beg their song. Let them decide what growth there'll be and render up your healing intent for them to use, and in this co-creation of your desire to heal and theirs to sing a world in song, the nature spirits will come forth to bind together that which has been sung and whole will be the garden state of Earth.

They appear to you as light, ethereal beings, yet this belies the activity of them. That they are called elementals is no accident and you would learn much of the importance of these creatures if you would ponder this other name. Nature spirits *are* elemental.

The elements are their vehicle and their parentage for it is through the elements that the devas work, just as it is through your body you work on Earth. There are those that are a direct product of the energies of nature you call the elements and these exist as raw expressions of the air, the fire, water etc., whatever in their raw form these phenomena are. But as each element has gathered, combined and functioned in more complicated form, as flowers, plants, trees, there you will find that sophisticated collaboration between the elements expressed as a sophisticated creature, uniquely combining the elements of its being as the plant has done. The two are inseparable just as your manifestation is a product of what you are.

They are driven not by individual but by collective will and only in the highest forms, like trees, will something like an individual will be found.

Because your bodies are made from the basic elements of Earth, combined of course in patterns of complexity unparalleled on Earth, you too are subject to a form of collective will, until you take command of these lesser modes and subject them to your higher Will. Let them 'run rampant' and you will always be at mercy of their whims, subject to the patterns of disease that mark a greater movement in the evolution and struggle of shaping Earth. But once commanded, these forces will obey your will with unswerving servitude. Remember though, that in this as in all other things you do, that the quality of your command comes back to you!

Crystalline Form

Crystals are solidified light. When this is truly understood, the power that formed them in the heart of the Earth can be unleashed. The power of a crystal comes not from its chemical arrangement for that is the *expression* of its power, not the source. Far more than the current power of even the smallest crystals will be realised when the question of light is understood.

Light transports the electric fire of the universe. In the crystal it remains in its purest form, unbent, not as in the other forms of matter. In the crystal the light is a direct arrangement of consciousness, the purest in matter there can be next to man as he *will* be. This is why crystals are such good transmitters of thought energy. Their molecules are arranged in a sequence and structure that allows clear passage of the consciousness that wishes to use them as storage, transmission or amplification of its thought energy into many manifold forms on this plane.

When man understands the directness of the channels set up by crystalline form he will realise how to direct his own thought energy and multiply it into form. Man is now sufficiently advanced to understand that since the crystal is a pure channel it must also be a perfect reflector for the energy running along those channels, therefore he must realise that as the crystal amplifies the energy it receives it will inevitably return in kind and amplitude the quality of the energy it received. Do you not see now why the power crystals of Atlantis were the means, if not the seed of its glory and destruction?

The violet devas work with you on this plane to produce the structure called forth by your desire to manifest a thought. Blue is the structure of the world but violet is the knowledge required to behold it, to convert the thought to form. This is why faith can move mountains because it sets up clear channels down which its light can pass and which cannot but obey the consciousness that commands it.

Crystals record. Their matrix of ordered molecular geometry is such that it must reflect the ordered patterns of the physical universe and therefore, the paths down which that history has travelled. Just as the arrangement of solar cells will 'record' and 'transmit' the character of the sun, the crystal holds and transmits a pattern imprinted upon it when its matrix is subjected to impulses of light just as a computer is 'imprinted' with information from an electrical current.

All 'events' that take place, do so at some level or other of light and are 'captured' or 'recorded' by whatever instrument is so constructed as to be compatible with that pattern of light. Thoughts are 'events' that emit greater or lesser levels of light or in the case of that which you call 'evil' apparently negative levels of light.

When you learn to travel the pathways of light (which remember also has sound) that a crystal holds by its inherent composition, you will access the information contained therein, just as you currently access the electrical information held within the 'pattern' of the computer's matrix you call circuitry.

Great Lords of consciousness have worked with crystal form. Thus each crystal kind is created as a resonance of a type of thought. That is why you will always find in the crystal world an aspect of the whole, an aspect perhaps that you seek to understand or to help supply you what you think you lack. The higher on your path you go, the greater help you will find there, and the greater tools are reserved for those skilled enough to use them. So it is with crystals. Do not use them if you are not equal to the task. As you learn and seek a greater knowing, so the greater stones will find you, for the Law is that like attracts like.

Crystal structures bind the very fabric of the Earth. What is clay but crystal? And even in the dark, gems unmined hold light not unleashed upon an unsuspecting world.

Know this especially, that crystals will not solve your problems, nor even help to light your way if you do not first hold the desire to see, and deep in your hearts wish to understand. Most of all, they will teach you to learn aright what and whom you choose to serve, for they are not mutable to your desire but reflectors and amplifiers of it, proclaiming loudly back at you, the measure of your thought. If your desire is of harm and selfishness, so will these precious gems return these qualities to you. If your touch is pure they will transform that touch for you and shine it back in light along the subtle structure of your being, that you may see clearly and feed directly on the quality of your thought. Learn to sing a crystal and find our secret, thine.

The Goblet

The goblet is a sign of Life. The fluid it contains moves not except within the cup as life moves not except within the One. To drink, whether of body or spirit is to partake of Life, to let Life flow through the channels of the body or the channels of the soul.

The cup is rounding, trying to be a sphere, the top open, as you must be, open to the Will divine that asks you drink the shining waters flowing from eternal Mind.

The fluid can also be poisoned, thus whatever you drink of, will your life and body be. Drink of the cup of hate and hate will fill you of hatefulness. Drink of the cup of fear and it will seep through every crack of your soul until you cannot see except through its darkness, nor move for its paralysing of your veins.

The cup may change in appearance. Be not fooled by the beauty or simplicity of the outside form. Look carefully at what liquid is contained within its walls. The appearance of the shell is like a doctrine, dressed up to fool the senses and appeal to the brain. But look inside, what does this doctrine's cup contain? Is it Life unspoken, or just a prattling spate of words chasing round and round an empty cup, a chalice of gold beloved of man but meaning naught of God and telling less of Him than the flowing forest stream where you might drink and know His Life, with nothing but the cupping of your own hands to hold Him, the One Life, your life.

Many have sought the cup, the grail, in physical reality—a spring of liquid life, an object of historical accuracy, the one that holds the 'blood' of Christ and many other such material echoes of a spiritual reality. Always, the personality and mind of man seeks to find through his physical senses that which cannot be sensed in the outer, but only grasped by the inner. Think long on the word *in*sight and much will reveal itself to you of the nature of different 'realities'. Talismans are the outward reminder of the inner reality, not the inner reality itself. Yet it is true that objects in the physical world can exhibit in themselves the Light of some spiritual majesty, but it is always the spiritual and not the object that owns the majesty.

When the grail cup is broken, the shards will lie useless on the ground and the liquid quench the thirst of a parched Earth, but only for a little while. When the thirst comes once more, the grail cup is no more and the ground of your life is dried and thirsty once more. But when the 'goblet,' 'grail,' 'cup' is rightly understood, then will the seeker seek no more and the lost river of Life be found. Then will the human seek no more in the phantom world of Earth for liquids of everlasting power, foods or objects of magical intent, but will give out Life itself to all things, and all things shall in turn give Life back to him.

Have we not told you, again and again, that God is Life in *all* things and as such, how can God not be the Life of you? Cups, goblets, talismans, sacred ornaments and all such things are echoes of the singer's song. Enjoy them, revel in their beauty if you will, but seek their singer, not their song.

What happens in the physical plane does not affect the spiritual planes in so far as the *action* of the physical plane is the result of a wave formed by conscious thought. Your state of consciousness does of course affect the level at which the consciousness takes place. It is in this sense that what the personality accomplishes in any life affects the Life experience of the soul.

Intent is a quality of soul, thus it is at the level of intent that the consciousness of the personality impinges on the life of the soul. So raise yourself and praise those who have raised themselves. And when you send out gratitude it is received by higher planes as well, for it is itself a higher vibration, therefore must it register in those higher planes.

The fluid in the cup is you, its casing the physicality produced by the 'thinking' that you do. Thus those who live solely on the planes of spirituality have vested interest in this fluid life of man. To participate in raising the consciousness of man is to be uplifted, for all partake in the same fluid, Life.

Do you not see then how it is possible for one great and mighty Master to take on and transmute the consciousness of a multitude of men? And do you not realise how the raising of your own consciousness will raise that of other men? You cannot 'bring down' those in higher spirituality than you, for they are above the influence of the dark unless they choose, regrettably, to descend. Yet they must know what it is you do, as a parent must see how the tiny infant learns to stand. At any level of your consciousness you affect those in that level with you. If you shine a light on a glass, does it not light up all the wine?

Yes, the fluid of the cup is you, but it is *all* of Life and other things that are *all* Life beside you, and fair indeed is the life lived in the clearest waters of My fountain. Love of all things is Love of God. It is His fluid the cup contains.

Love

The quickest way to calm the mind is to fill the heart with Love, not 'love' of the loins nor 'love' of fear, but the Love of He that *is*, the Love untouched that changes not. It contains compassion but has no pity for pity sees not divinely and therefore raises not that which is pitied. To love divinely is to waiver not and requires no courage for courage is a need to answer fear and how can Love have fear?

To love divinely is a blissful state, creating peace so totally devoid of falsity that nothing else exists outside its hallowed halls, for it is Truth. It seems to move, spreading ever outward as a radiant glow, but actually is still, for peace is Love and Love is always still. Its rays of Light move out in fingers warmer than the Sun, in beauty greater than the Earth, for this is Christ, the Love of the divine which dwells in every heart of man to raise him to that place of peace where strength is gentle and all troubles cease, disappeared like fear of dark at morn.

Evil is the measure of a man's distrust of Love. Love knows no evil. It cannot, because it is the state of being we call God or Oneness. To have any evil in it, Love would have to work against itself. Yet God must contain all possibility, including the possibility of evil. But as we have seen, the possibilities arising from God are apparent since God is indivisible and cannot be divided and therefore cannot be something, that is, evil, which it is not. Evil and Love cannot co-exist. How then, does that which man calls evil appear to be? To be the potential of all that there is, God must have free will to play with those potentials, and since nothing *is* without God, free will must be inherent within those creations of God that are expressing that potential. The manifested aspect of God, in this case man, is therefore free to play with the idea granted by free will, of something opposed to itself; evil or *not*-Love, to be more accurately put. Yet *not*-Love, in the Reality that God is, cannot in Truth exist, since Love is one of the essential attributes of God. Evil is therefore, at worst an unpleasant game mankind insists on playing until it is tired of such gruesome sport. For what can be more gruesome than the attempt to be what one is not?

Such confusion has arisen from the words, 'Turn the other cheek'. No 'blow' can in Truth be received when one stands in active outpouring of Love. When your being is filled by Love flowing out, how can 'evil' flow in? Think on this, know this, and be this and naught can bound you in the world of form. For when you stand in Love, you stand in the path of God and it cannot be otherwise except that God move through you. Then do you stand above all men but judge them not and in your presence they will be healed, for all is healed in the presence of God.

Often man has attributed to God that which he interprets as evil, acts he sees as revengeful or of 'divine wrath'. In this he has overlooked the working out of the Law of God, that for every apparent movement within the Oneness of God, there must be an equal and complementary reaction to mirror it, completing its completeness, and what is attributed to God is often no more than the wrecking of the consequences of his own thought and doing upon man, the initiator himself.

Man also does not understand the 'destructive' nature of God. When the greatest degree of physicality is being expressed, such as in the world of Earth which your senses experience, two forms cannot occupy the same space and time. A form therefore is 'destroyed' to make 'room' for another to take its place as the momentum of God's movement continues inevitably to express itself. To the mortal mind, this seems wantonly destructive, but only because those who cannot get above the ground see nothing of the landscape beyond their own height. Were you to rise to a consciousness that can comprehend the greater mind, it would not seem destructive at all, since you would see that the form of the thing is not the thing itself.

To live in closer harmony with the true nature of oneself is to live with greater illumination. Illumination is understanding. The further from the source of its own movement an idea is, the 'heavier,' the more physical, it becomes. To be closer to the source, that which thinks, or God, is to become lighter, thus it is called enlightenment, for the divine is total knowledge and understanding, Light.

The nature of God is Love, without an understanding of which man is doomed to misery. It has no desire, for it flows ever outward. It has no needs for it is complete unto itself. Can you not see the difference between your desire, which you have called 'love', and God which *is* Love?

The Will of God is power. Nothing can stand in the way of that which God has ordained. Yet man has ever misjudged this, thinking many things to be God's Will which are simply the natural consequences of levels of being and chosen lines of thought. Not until the next age of your sun will mankind begin to understand *that* nature called the Will of God and so far off is this in the enlightenment of Earth that it is useless to attend to it now.

The lesson now is Love. To understand its selfless nature, to subjugate the little will of self to the greater Will of

Love, is the task of now. To put the heart, centred in the consciousness of God, before all else, is the need of mankind. For Love has its own energy and asks nothing. It flows out but is constantly renewed. It judges not because it recognises nothing but itself.

Love is the basis of all power for nothing else *is*. Of course it overcomes anything seen as lack because in it there is no lack. It strangles nothing because it lets everything be. Of itself it hurts nothing because it is gentleness indeed, but those who flee in terror from its beauty may hurt themselves in their scrambling from its all pervading seeping into their hearts.

When Love is pouring from your heart centre, nothing can assail you, for what can find its way through outflowing Love? It shields you not, as if there was something to protect you from, for it recognises nothing but the Reality of Truth, and when you pour it forth from you, you act with God, for He is naught but Love. So think it not a means to any end, for that is mere desire and will reward only in the hollow measure of its temporal nature. But Love that *is* the Life of God pouring from the heart of man, will put you in experience of God where things of the physical plane are seen for what they are, as flitting stops across a stage of plays, but you will stand invincible upon another plane.

Love is creative but does not act. How can this be? It *appears* to you that creation is action, but in Reality nothing exists but a state of being. In your worlds and in the higher, *all* aspects of God are creative, Love is but one of these.

The difficulty for you is that because you have recognised an aspect of God's nature, in this case Love, you have separated it in your mind when in Truth it cannot be. In Truth all the aspects of God are *one* nature. To see them as Love, Truth, Beauty, or any such as these is to have barely a little understanding and regretfully man has but yet only a little understanding of things such as these.

When you attain a state of Love, it must of its nature give the power of Creativity since as we have said, Love Creates. It may end up creating something that results in a form, an event in your world of echoes, but if you dwell on all that has been said before on the workings of the nature of God or the divine, then you will realise that all which seems to move is actually still.

Love, as it is divine, is the highest of what seem to you emotions. The emotions you experience day to day are simply the result of man's attempt to imitate the non-moving action of creation. They are an attempt to play out the part without the whole. That is why they have ensnared you in a tumult of muddled indecisiveness and fears. When you look into the great 'emotion' of God—Love—you find all the nature of divinity is yours because divinity is *One* and not one of its natures or attributes can be separated from the rest. So it is that when you have Love you have power and wisdom, intelligence and force, and mighty indeed is that which is accomplished in Love.

Do you not see how as children of Love you must *be* Love indeed? Do you not see how all the attributes of God must be yours and if God is Love, so must you be? Slowly, step by step, leave your emotions you erected in limitation of His greatness behind. Then, in non-concentration on the false, will divinity in Truth reveal itself in you. It does not need to be sought because it is always 'there'. It does not need to be attained, it is what you truly are. It does not need to be longed for because longing will distance it, assuming there lie barriers between you and it.

Yet you are told to seek to find. To seek the divine is to turn away from inventions of your own. Turn around and Love *is*. Turn around and power *is*. Turn around and all there is to know is God *is*. Such is Love, and you need seek it not, but stop your wailing fantasy of gloom and you will find it, wrapping you inside its wings in peace and security and understanding that only the Love which is divinity can bring.

Capture that which changes not, by feeling with the heart the Christ in thee. Let the heart be your eyes, it will see in place of all the temporariness the world transports before your eyes, a ray of light, a shard of joy, a piece of Truth in place of lies. The heart, the heart! To all your fellow-man belongs the heart. To all the kingdoms found beside you, belongs your heart. Let your lips be silent but your heart speak to all. Put your heart before your eyes that you might see nothing except through its sight, and hardest of all, let your heart come out before your ears that you might, but only with compassion, filter sound through Love. Speak not unless your heart's before your mouth.

Love never binds nor restricts. It never commands what will be or not be done, it simply is there for the lover to pleasure with or no. So you see Little One, you have not been cast out but let go as you will, and the Father's Will is nothing more than Love. Such peace is there in this, and you thought it so demanding! Nay, 'tis Bliss, just bliss softly rising on its wings. Wings are Love. They hold you up, support you, take you lightly anywhere you want to go. They both protect you and make you bold, shelter you and set you free. Is that not Love?

How could we not give you freedom totally if we did not love you with such faith in you? How could we let you traverse the gardens of the universe unfettered but never unguarded or unsupported by loving hands? When in striving you are hurt, it does not bring us sorrow, for what is hurt and how can it alter Love?

Love is a state of being from which a motion flows. It is not itself an act though acts may rise from it. Love does not act, it *is*, and since it does not alter, how can it be changed by a seeming circumstance like hurt? It is the essential you that is the object of our Love, not a motion or an action; merely states of mind, imagined sometimes by you to be yourself.

You stumble and grasp, seeing not what you grasp onto. You search for Love but find it not in God. Seek not Love therefore, but *be* it, for with Love, the Light of God will shine your way and His Will guide your steps through both night and day.

Freedom

Freedom lies not in the things of this world but is the freedom from them. It is granted not by others but by the self. He who has attained true freedom has it regardless of his Earthly circumstances. He can be imprisoned by tyrants and yet have more freedom than his captors. He can have no refinement of dress or demeanour yet be more free than they who can choose from all the world's greatest fashion and loveliest accents.

Freedom means different things at different levels of awareness. To the unawakened man it means physical freedom and then, as he 'advances,' the desire moves up to the emotional/mental centres and ideological freedom is sought. When the higher mind is activated, (rather than the intellect which is still strongly linked to the emotional) when spiritual awakening occurs and the human seeks Truth beyond sectarian ideologies, (political or religious) then the freedom sought becomes less easy to articulate for it moves into a desire for freedom from all that has hitherto been valued. Broadly speaking, it could be said to be freedom from attachment to the things of the physical world and the socially conditioned values which have more to do with the smooth regulation of society than the nature of spiritual being.

Once freedom from the world is gained, or beginning to be wholly grasped, then even greater freedoms open before the realising soul and the seeker begins to desire freedom to exist with full awareness on all the planes. And beyond this there are freedoms more, far out of reach of the possibility of your understanding, and it is enough that you learn to walk and run before you flap your wings and fly!

As with all things of aspiration, freedom is a state of being, born of knowledge of the Truth. They who have attained the freedom of Truth are not touched by popularity or lack, abundance or apparent poverty, and they are free to give their lives in service for they have truly 'overcome the world'.

How often have great battles for freedom been fought and won by men, only to be fought again in a later generation? Does this not tell you that the freedom gained was transitory and therefore not freedom at all? Yet these battles were 'necessary' to stay a tyrants hand and lead humanity to want freedom in Truth and not just seeming. For tyrants are the side of self that wants control as the little self of man does seek control, and not until the higher has subsumed this desire for control can the tiny self concede and render up its painful ways for freedom's gain.

Day by day, hour by hour, must the motive of your desire be checked. And only when confusion ceases and you truly know the difference between control by self and Will of God, will the world transform for you and all you touch will bloom as soul gains mastery of self and freedom from opposition to Oneness is gained. Oneness is the ignorance of separation, a blindness to divisions so loved in your world, a non-attachment to status keys, wealth, poverty, intellectual gain, cleverness or a glib tongue's loquacious refrain!

Oneness *is* freedom. The freedom lies not in that which is created but in the uncreated, which is the potential of limitless possibility. Once attention is focused on what is manifested from that potential, limits (and therefore lack of freedom) are placed on being, regardless of how exciting or varied what has been created might be, because to focus on what has been created is to wander down one path, necessarily at that instant, to the exclusion of all others. That is the nature of that mode of being, and this limited existence is the experience of all unenlightened human beings.

It is only when you can experience the uncreated potential of the One that you can experience true freedom, for then the inexpressible *all* is known. There is a sense of course, in which no human being can know such freedom, because in that instant he is no longer 'human' but divine. He has ceased to attend to the motion of thought and identified with the source of all thought, still, uncreated *is-ness*.

Freedom happens when you cease to dwell on the jumble of pre-conditioned social views that stand in the way of your being the natural you. Freedom is not a licence to trample over the needs of others, for the truly free are harmless. Neither does it lessen one's responsibility to serve, rather it is itself service for by losing self-interest you automatically serve.

The freedom to be what one *is* in the universe is hard won and yet so easy that once realised the paradox dissolves and joy fills all the spaces where conflict once arose. Freedom does not come in the running away from duty or avoidance of long application of effort, but through detachment of desire for self-gratification, and recognising instead that the soul effort is for group good, for only by serving the whole can the part be fulfilled.

Always the explanation of Truth must seem a riddle to the unwise but as the seeker gains in wisdom, (and thus in freedom from the world) so the explanation becomes experienced and riddling words like 'he who loses his life shall gain it,' become clear. Always the 'I' refers to God; the higher Self, the soul of you, the first stage to regaining the Freedom of God itself, for again, what can you be except God itself, the 'I' in you that has never left you but will stay with you even to the 'end of the world' for it *is* you.

Unless you practise daily an aspect of Truth, Freedom never lights your hours nor sets your heart ablaze with Life. Nor shall the wings of your soul gain access to the deepest reaches of the Earth to raise those beings who dwell beside you as grass and flowers, bees, or rock and stream. As you travel there beside them your awareness of the God within will lift them up and set them free, for Love is ever the mover and it is Love that gives you wings and non-attaching, sets you free.

As you identify with God, you identify with the God in all things and this recognition is Love itself. We cannot talk of freedom without talking of Love, we cannot discover Love until the tiny self is seen for what it is. When we talk of Love and Freedom and Self, we discover there is the One that moves not, but that its thinking appears to be movement. In that infinite potential that God is, we discover that God's thinking seems to move in waves of colour, light and sound and so we find the dualities of what appears to be. Then the opposites dissolve each other, behind them Truth, standing alone for us to see. In the forming worlds many stages are wrought until the spherical perfection of manifested being comes to be.

Can you not see how all we have discussed in these pages is like the opening of a flower, so vast and beautiful and wonderful, you had not even dreamed of its likeness? And can you not see that we have been buzzing through the petals of this beautiful flower and yet all the angles from which we have viewed it, were just that, angles on the same flower?

So when you ponder, and read again, you will find all that wanders in your mind behind the words, fitting together all these parts linking to the greater whole, each part in holographic truth, being also whole.

Such are the riddles of Truth which reveals itself not in dissection but in apprehension, constantly moving farther away as you run after it as any child knows who tried to catch a feather or a butterfly. But stand still and the butterflies of Truth will come after you and settle in your heart, and you will not need to seek, for the lotus flower of Truth will bloom upon your crown and the Light of every son shine forth from your face, for you will have found Truth in you, and Truth is God.

The Self

Ponder on these questions. What are you? What is the nature of your being? And what is your relationship to all that appears to be in the world with you? You identify yourself within the world according to the functions which you serve—as businessman or baker, waiter or teacher, father, mother, brother, sister or any number of other parts you choose to play. We say you are a child of God, but it means almost nothing to you, since the nature and even the very existence of God is often in dispute. You are as a man who lives in a box, not knowing his box sits in a vast meadow, aglow with flowers, and the meadow within a vaster land, within a world, and even then, 'tis only a tiny speck in a vaster universe.

We will use two ways of describing self, not because of any 'reality' they might have but to show you two modes of being you have open to you. One, with a small 's' is the mode of the personality, the consciousness that sees itself as separate from everything else. The other, with a capital 'S' we use to show the mode of higher Self or, (for the purpose of this discussion) soul. This division into two is simply useful, that is all.

There are several keys to revealing the Self. First of these is humility, for only by humility of the self can Love, the second key, be unveiled. The self has not Love sufficient to bridge the chasm between illusion and Truth. But the

Self, which knows only Love as its power and source, moves ever in Love. In humility there is submission without weakness. Submission to divine Will and reason is the third key to Self.

The tiny self fights constantly for what it thinks it has, whereas in truth it has nothing for it tries to base its power outside of God, and how can there be in truth, anything outside of God? The belief in 'not God' *is* the illusion of the world, not to be resisted for it *is* not, not to be overcome for it has no power, and all that maintains it is belief.

The keys to the Kingdom are so light they weigh nothing, so illumined they cannot be seen, and those who possess them grasp them not but allow them to shine forth in radiant declaration. Seek not the keys to the Kingdom, but the attributes of those who know they dwell within. Humble thy tiny self, not in shame or degradation, but with neutral deference to what *is* and humility will find itself in Love.

Both the self and the Self control the body because both are consciousness, but they are consciousness of different sorts or qualities, one divine and the other the construction of a free will. Problems arise when the constructed self has ceased to follow the natural laws of divine Will, resulting in struggle and conflict which directly, through the nervous system and chemical reaction, affect the body.

Remember that all the universe is sound and sound moves matter into patterns. Your thoughts and emotions are the songs your consciousness sings. They sing your body into different states, according to the quality of the song. Since an effect never leaves its cause, your thoughts remain to affect you throughout your chain of command from the source of your thinking to its apparent end product, your body and the outer appearances of your life.

Oh happy is he who has ceased to construct his life against the tide of divine reason, who has ceased to react to whims of the world and the thought forms of others. Such a one as this places no barriers of his own assumptions between Life and self, instead allowing Self, which resides in Life, to run his thoughts.

No hurt can ever be redressed, revenge does not exist, and forgiveness is the relinquishment of blame. Such are the jewels in the crown of Self, for Love, which is outpouring, allows nothing back in except itself.

Compassion is the acceptance of Love as the ultimate source of power and is the application of Love to any appearance of hurt.

Teach your children the cause and effect of their lives and you give them the keys to the Kingdom. Teach them that their power lies in Self and not in the acts of others nor the circumstances of the world and you will have nations free of strife who covert not each other's power nor tear apart the planet's beauty in the quest for reasonless junk whose true cost man seldom knows.

The personality takes pleasure in measuring one of you against another as if there were truly some difference of 'rank'. It is true that you are all at different stages of unfoldment, but the unfoldment is a question of awareness, not of essence. It is difficult for you to grasp that which does not fit the linear pattern of your thought when trying to understand the relationship of soul to personality, master to student and 'brother' to 'brother'.

From the point of God wherein you lie, each is created equal to the other because all are God, but each expresses that aspect of God which is exclusively itself, even though as part of an indivisible whole each exists within the other. But in the expression of that individual aspect of God that each one is, each springs forth in a complex cluster of waves propelled by the source or essence of what it is in the mind of God. At no stage in this extension from the source, can it not have the attributes with which it began.

How can a ribbon of water leaping in a fountain not be the same water from which it leaped forth? When you understand this you understand the words of Christ, that 'What is mine is thine'. Just as with the fountain, some drops of water might be flung and separated from the rest though they are still water, so it can feel that you are separate from the rest or source of you, and the personality seems to lie, for aeons, alone.

However, the soul has force, more like magnetism than water, though water too, when meeting with its kind will quickly merge. This force—the magnetism of the soul—draws ever on its seemingly separated self, that struggling entity we call man, who, like a child that thinks itself lost, cannot stand tall enough to see its parent close behind. But the small self remember, has the attributes of the soul, and once it realises this is so, can exert its own magnetism to reach for and re-establish connection to the soul. Like the water of the fountain, it does, after its flinging forth *that* life, tumble back again into the source of the fountain.

Your task then is to re-establish your connection to the soul which in truth is never broken, we have merely said it so for purposes of explication. Can you not see now, why the little will must be brought in subjugation beneath the Will of God, or soul?

What appears to be disintegration and death is only the return or collapse of a waveform. Once it has reached the extent of the energy that sent it forth, it must, by its very nature return. The amount of power or force that thrust it forth in the first place determines the length of what you call its 'life'. It is consciousness that throws forth bands of waves that appear to you as objects in your world. This applies to your bodies too. Hence they reach a peak and then collapse and decay but always behind their propulsion is you and that which co-creates your body with you. The tone and quality of your consciousness does therefore profoundly affect the effects your body shows to you, but only those who have attained a high degree of spiritual mastery can entirely influence the outcome of that which is their body.

The waveform that springs forth as you, has no end for it is God, which has no end. The body you identify as you is flung forth with but a little power, in the mighty scheme of things, for it need not last longer than the chosen cycle takes for you to learn. When this movement is mastered, the soul in glory of its expression can journey forth in confidence of never losing its farthest flung part to the seduction of the experience. It gains control and moves about the manifested worlds as trailing rays of Light that dance its tune, singing its Creator's song to every world that each world might know God fully.

Thus for each soul the journey of being is infinite joy, as God has no limit to potential and in that still point of Light do all the worlds explode.

Epilogue

To God

I am lost in wonderment at the vastness of what You are
Without You, I have no being
Without You, nothing is

Let me find my love for You
Before my awe diverts my feelings into non-existence,
And I lose, for fear of its greatness, the glimpse of You

And every time the little things of the world tangle up
    my heart,
Let me remember You,
And they shall disappear as rain upon a droughted
    ground.

Book II

Prophets speak to the time in which they see,
and even prophets
must move on to higher things.

Introduction

The subjects of this book are interrelated. More than this they are in fact all the same topic. Truth is One and words are at best a linear representation of what is not linear but 'holographic'. Each topic therefore, is just a window showing a different view of the same Truth.

Because humankind is easily blown about by change, a different mood will find Truth in a different way. Delve therefore as the mood takes you but practise diligently the wisdom herein and it will not be mood but knowledge that rules your life and orders the reactions of your day.

We have used the term 'God' because it is important to be clear about what this word means. Ever man will argue the use of words as if words have some reality of themselves whereas they are only symbols of a greater meaning. Right now, humankind needs to understand the greater meaning behind this word that he may see the falsity of division between the belief groups of his world. When you see the word 'God' in this text therefore, take the broader meaning as it is presented here, not the narrow confines of what you have been taught that word should mean. Do not limit God to your small idea of Him!

When you can use not words, but the speech of your mind with other minds, you will have no need to restrict the concept of God to 'He' or 'It' or 'She'. But for now, read not the personal 'He' literally. You yet need this personal noun to relate God to the individuality of you and will learn that God is both personal and impersonal, but in fact his personal manifestation *is* you.

This book will give you many keys if you will but let it. Hold it not tightly in your mind but let your heart wander round its words and free your mind to travel farther than your known world, into the door of distant realms. Ever the key is your intent, to let the greater God lead you or to stay confined within the walls of man's convention set by men of past religion, righteous in their way but tiny in their scope when shown against the opportunities of your expanding minds today.

Many agonies do the spiritually brave suffer over the dualism of materialism and mind. But this is only temporary misunderstanding of cause and effect. To deny your part in the world is to misunderstand the principles of cause and effect, and when you understand the relationship of consciousness to materiality you will no longer abdicate your responsibility but grasp your lives with Love and Will, and truly then will spirit manifest on Earth.

As you see the world, so it is for you. To understand and move beyond this truism is the prize of soul communication and only when you truly move beyond it do you become really useful in the world. Usefulness, service—these are the prizes that emerge unlooked for when you understand how to *be* only that which in pure essence you are. From such understanding and practise grows desire, willingness and readiness to serve.

When you understand your being, you begin to serve Being itself. You cannot help it, it is automatic, because within Being there is in Truth no division, though there is distinction, until each has travelled by his own route to the same end, and he who serves Being must in the end be serving all.

Being is a state of grace. It is not a reward for good behaviour dished out by a judgmental God, but the state, the nature if you like, of a level of consciousness. God does not punish, but sets the Law, the framework by which worlds exist, and within which they have their form. Consequence, 'good' or 'bad,' follows naturally according to your understanding of and adherence to, those fundamental laws. All that is created by God *is* God, and it is not for man to judge, (according to his own social whim and interpretation) those which God creates in likeness of each other on any plane. All are at different stages of unfoldment in their understanding and their place in the working out of what man has called 'God's plan'.

The wise man loves, but discriminates wisely, understanding what is appropriate for those at different levels of awareness. The attainment of such wisdom is not acquired by social decree or appointment to high office, though high office may be the outcome of one's attaining wisdom. No, wisdom comes when the ability to love is tempered by knowledge, when all the subtle bodies of a man are pure and wholly aligned, not to his Earthly kings of selfishness or greed or ambitious desire, but to the master teacher of his soul under whose tutelage he grows. This master and the other 'lesser' teachers of your soul do not recruit, but they wait always in readiness for your call and the attunement of your consciousness to a level whereon you may feel, see, know or hear their response.

Patience children Mine! You cannot in your world of time, jump in a day from desire to mastery, any more than you can run the fastest race without the skill or training. If you would know your teachers on the inner planes, training and skill is indeed necessary, but be not discouraged at what I say for right practise must always bring its just reward. That is the Law, that the nature of the intent will guide the activity that leads to the complement, the attainment of the intent.

Diligent practise, intelligent discrimination of thought, will bring results and steadily the fruits of lifetimes will be yours How can they not be? There is no failure in God's language, for all must return in consciousness to God again, since they are themselves God, and nothing truly leaves its creator, no matter how far and how dangerously some seem to have travelled in darkness of hate, or lust for power, or personal despair.

So, aspirants of Light, be strong, for nothing but the Light dwells within the innermost heart of you. And give not your power to *any* thing that diminishes or hides this Light from you. And when a man-made law attempts to hide the Light of one to advantage another, it is not God's law but man's indulgence in the personal ambition of man. And when one offends against the Light of another, he cannot really in Truth diminish that Light, yet the error of his thinking must be understood by him, and society must be at pains to correct unrelentingly until the man himself can see and know and understand the error of his ways. The love and respect of each other must always be the aim, but Love is not weak, it is wise, and tolerates not the criminal nor the foolish, but sets both upon the path of understanding, the one to turn about its desire, the other to bring intelligence and discrimination into the life.

Love is not a weak acceptance but a burning flame that works in consort with wisdom and God's Will, and thus is God's plan advanced and all the myriad worlds return themselves to heaven. Heaven, and what is heaven? Heaven is a place of knowing beyond which lie greater halls of knowing, and the journey ever higher does indeed have end where it began, inside the One creating 'I' that moves not, but sits behind all manifested things, as your own flame moves not but sits as manifested God within the depths, beyond which there is nothing else, at the uttermost centre of you.

Wisdom is never about selfishness, yet knowledge of Self is an essential ingredient in that intricate and distinguished web that is the subtle makeup of the wise. Put aside your previous perception and read what is written. Look carefully for that which cautions and balances, urging you to reason divinely beyond the muddied waters of other people's repetitions of yet still other people's teachings. This book is about learning to discriminate, to tune the inner ear to the subtleties of being, that you may learn which part of you it is that speaks to you, that you may know the solidity of the source of your own soul, then to know that source the source of all that is, supplier of a never-ending stream of Light for you, unbroken by what would before have been cause of much distress.

Slowly, but steadfastly, you may fly through the storms of inconsistency and bring at last all the diverse, warring parts of you together, aligned upon the mirror of your soul that you may know your being in all its varied aspects, and put at last to greater use that part of you whose footsteps tread the Earth. Yet all the while your mind's aligned with heaven that the Light of higher planes be funnelled down, that you may *know*, not just in some romantic way, what being is; a multitude of levels, yet a core unchanging, a multi-faceted jewel created by the splendour of God, yet a single bright Light that illuminates the dark that all may, at last, see once more.

The Soul

The question of the soul has bothered both wise and true men since time grew from timelessness and action flowered where only stillness had been. The answers are simple as Truth has always been. You reside first in the requited Stillness of God. Being Him your qualities are His. Set there in the Stillness of all the potential there is, you move not but simply are.

The idea of you desires expression and is achieved by exploration as the potential that you are 'moves out' to 'look back,' to see *all* that you are. This looking and exploring is not done in actual movement but in consciousness for consciousness is all you ever really are. Your 'life' then is 'your' consciousness exploring all that it is. So you can never really *do* to know yourself but only *be*. No matter how far you go in movement you cannot leave yourself 'behind' and can never therefore truly 'go outside' yourself to look at what you are. The 'journey of the soul' therefore is an experiment in knowing. Can you not see then why you can only 'find God' in the stillness of you and not in the tricksy, flickering movement that constitutes the outer world of man?

To know this is not to deny but to understand, not to withdraw into mystic solitude, but to stand on a rock in the midst of shifting sand. At any moment it is where your consciousness attends that brings your experience to you. If it rests only on the moving world of echoes 'outside' of you then it will be bounced around by these sounds back and forth to each other. But if it remains fixed on the stillness within it knows who it is and remains unmoved by the confusion and doubt of other people's echoes.

Why is this so hard for you to do, to stay in that 'place' where there can be no judgement of a social measure for nothing is 'done' which requires it, where being is ever joyful for that is the nature of God and it is always so. Such dangerous ground lies across mortality! Quicksands of social reason, justifying all the plays that humans claim as 'right,' yet what rightness there would grow from consciousness of unity, from each standing on the rock of his own soul. When the consciousness stays on the rock of the soul, the flowers of one's thought bloom ever gentle, answering not the winds of change with despair at some kind of loss, but feeling them not, and into the world blowing instead the gentle breeze of knowing that each standing beside you is God.

Why attend to the 'journey' of the soul? It has no journey but only *is*. Action is an effect of consciousness, it rises out of thought. Agonise then not over your actions but attend to the basis of your thought. Fix firmly the basis of your thought in the consciousness of your soul and 'right' action will flow. How can it not? Leave aside all intellectual games and philosophies. These are but distractions. Be still, even in movement, still. Let the dance of your life come from the soul. Seek not to find it but know it. Drop all the baggage built by your effort. Those who stay in God *know*, and the knowing requires no effort. Frustration only comes from effort not directed by the soul. Truth knows no other beside itself so the truth of the soul is not tied by conflicting views or struggles of the so-called 'real' world.

Cause and effect are the natural, inescapable consequence of thought because thought imprints on or 'moves' the substance of being. When your consciousness never loses its link with itself, (the soul) then its consequences—the action coming from its thought—must have the qualities of the soul. Phantoms always fly in the face of Truth. Weakness crumbles under its strength and the unreal dissolves as fantasy in the Light of its knowing.

When obsessed with doubt, go back to your soul. When tied to remorse, seek the Truth of your soul. What is your soul? It is a word for what you are. How will you know when you have found it? Of all the things you think you are it is the only one which you *truly* are. It moves not.

Your soul is the multi-mirrored Selfhood of you. It is the individual expression of God which you are. But there are higher joinings for the soul, that you might become part of a greater soul, just as your personality, the tiny self of you becomes one with your soul, for when the personality ceases to function except with direction from the soul, it is no longer an independent individual 'you,' but truly the implement of your higher Self in the world.

First, man must realise he is not human but a soul. Second, he must realise that his spirit *is* Spirit, the same Spirit in which all move and have their being. Such revelations confine themselves not to the consciousness of you but to the consciousness of other 'products' of Spirit in the world with you. Division must dissolve eventually between all that constitutes the world and you, and the beingness that produces appearance of both planet and you, eventually reveal itself to you. The enlightened human knows that *as a personality,* he functions no more 'above' than do the cells and systems of his body function above himself, that he cannot in isolation revel in goodness since without the rest he *is* not, and goodness is the true nature of All.

Do you not see then, how the raising of consciousness must eliminate the barriers your 'journey' into individuation has produced to delude you? As you raise your consciousness to the great heights will know there is not you and other but only you. The 'you' is seen for what it is and that is One, and we call it 'God'. There is not really therefore in the world, a multitude of souls and you, but only God *expressed* as different 'things'.

Feelings are part of the sentience of being. At each level of consciousness they are limited or bound in quality by the nature and structure of the body that is the mechanism of their experience. Just as, if you travel in an enclosed vehicle you cannot feel the air rushing past you, so, when experiencing through a particular body, certain experiences are not available to you. Thus the experiences you call emotions —which are felt by the lower receptive body, the emotional body or aspect of your consciousness—are very different and limited compared to that which is available to the feeling aspect of the soul body's equivalent, the sentient body.

Freedom from restriction of the emotions of the human 'body' level comes not through a restructuring of that lower body which must be limited by its realm and function, but by the attention of your consciousness to the higher sentience of the soul, by continually functioning from this higher plane until the lower is *consumed* by the higher and the emotional body ceases to dictate, then the life of the soul can proceed unhindered, even, apparently, on the Earth plane. Great can be the struggle to bring about this freedom and great is the confusion as the human being strives to know the difference between his human emotions and the sentience of the soul.

The narrow bridge beyond the crown is the 'umbilicus' through which the human must contact his soul. As with a physically narrow bridge in your world, you cannot cross it if the load you carry is too wide for its entrance. Such is the bulky personality that must be left behind to cross this narrow bridge to the freedom of the soul's realm. Eventually, even your physical body can be directed by the greater commander across this bridge to the soul, and the lower, being of no more use and unused, withers, burns, and disappears.

At the level of the soul, sentience and knowledge are effectively the same thing. At the human level, the divergent activities of feelings, intellect and body response are the function aspects or outcomes of separation thinking. Legends and mythologies have been built to help mankind understand how it is that he seems to have fallen to disintegration, experiencing being as disjointed aspects of a life separated from the Life of all. It is no more than a mode of thinking that has become a habit, dangerous only in the suffering it causes, yet it poses no danger to Truth. How can it? The man who by his nature and circumstance concludes that the world and life in general hates and conspires against him, no more changes the Truth that Life just *is* despite his view of it, than does a leaf falling from an autumnal tree change the power of the wind by its fall.

'Separation' is itself a human emotion, not a fact of Truth. Its children are many for each creative activity spawns itself unchecked until the thought creating it ceases to send it forth. It is not a punishment of God, which simply does not recognise its unreality, knowing Itself to be all there truly is. The suffering that returns to man from his practise of separative thinking is nothing more than the consequences of the thinking itself. If you would be free then of the suffering 'separation' brings, you must examine honestly the habits of your thinking and abandon them in favour of the Truth that there are not many things, but only the one thing, which we have named 'God'.

Separation thinking spawns many glamorous things that attract and entrap the emotions of man. Why? Because they are fabrications of the emotions of man. They are fears and worries and greeds, insecurities and anything of any other name that you have invented which is not of the twin nature of God in action, Love and divine Will. So complete is this fabrication of the emotions of man that some that are of your invention and not of God's seem noble and right to you. Only close examination of the feelings behind your intent can reveal the truth of their nature to you, and only replacement of your habits by the surrender of your tiny self to your soul corrects this separation thinking and opens the realms of heaven to you.

Your soul is the individuation of you, not the ultimate cause or destination of you. The souls of each of you are joined on even higher planes in a Oneness of being, even as you look upon your different personality attributes as expressions of you, not as entities separate from you. So it is in the higher planes, looking upon the individuation you see 'down here' as you. But in the higher planes the many *are* a unity, looking not inward to each other as parts of a whole but 'they' have become one and *are* the functioning whole.

Mastery can be said to be a relinquishment of control, a dropping of the emotions of the lower expression of being for the higher 'emotion' of the soul, Love, and its directive, Will. You cannot truly *be* while you are trying to be something you are not. While you *seem* to be separate from other manifested things you cannot in Truth be separate from the Life, which behind their manifested form, they are.

The sentience of the soul is its experience of being. Not split nor compartmentalised but integrated and whole, aware of eternity for eternity is all it knows. Not static but aspiring still to the higher state of being is the unity that commands even the level of the soul. The key to your life now is soul communication. Without it you stumble around in the dark.

To stay in the Love of the soul is truly to bring heaven to each day, and being the 'prime mover' available to your world today, it can heal bodily ills and change political will. But it must be Love and not desire, unconditional and non-judging, of a strength and nature that overwhelms the petty, dissolving it as shadows must dissolve before the noon-day sun, as fear of night must disappear at dawn and as shelter is your safety in a storm.

It requires only practice, this non-exclusive Love. It is natural as your breathing, it could change your every day. It is the Truth, and it has no regrets. It contents you not with second best because you cannot contain it, it is all there is. To block it is death yet death cannot stop it. Hide from it and it will await you when you emerge. It lives in every bird and tree. It flies the butterflies and bees. It drives the night and wakens open every day. Become its conduit and death and illness will be swept away. Embrace it lovingly, give it gratitude and it will serve you brightly with chances, and richly with possibilities, not in order of your making but at bidding of a tune that comes from God.

The Personality

The personality is the most concrete form of your uniqueness. It is that part of you which has flung farthest into materiality and is therefore the most vulnerable to the experience of 'separation'. If you think of yourself as a continuous line or wave from the source (God) to your physical reality with that wave passing through many stages and types of awareness and solidity as it stretches between the source and its outermost extension, you can see that to access the higher parts of your being, (those closer to the source), you need to draw your attention away from your personality, which drives the physical, and place your awareness back up your wave in the direction of its source.

The will aspect that drives the personality is what we call the ego. A strong ego enables you to get things done in the world, but if allowed to dominate all the time it prevents you from having your worldly activity directed by higher aspects of your Self.

When you engage the heart, you engage the love aspect of the personality. The intellect with its interest in structures and systems distracts the mind, absorbing it in a closed world of its own making. Unfettered by the intellect, the mind can reach any level of consciousness, connecting one with the other, bringing inspiration from 'above' to co-ordinate and harmonise all aspects of being; the feeling (love), the physical (materialism or manifestation), and the *higher* mental planes that are unbounded by dogma or confined by structure (as you understand it.)

The challenge now is to stay connected intuitively, thus allowing the mental faculties to function as they should, as a means of access to all wisdom and higher thought, not to remain isolated, out to the side, engaged in the self-constructed mental games of the human plane, which have in the end no more lasting value than a sporting game. The higher intuition which is the proper realm of the mental body, directs the life in ways undreamed by the intellect, with a richness and breadth of experience of mind for which mind was in fact designed, and furthers the evolution of humankind quicker than anything of social importance the intellect can construct in its place.

The ego and the intellect are necessary aspects of the personality, but they are of little use, in fact can be counter productive, when not brought under the control, or subsumed by, the higher aspects of Will, Love and Intuition. To stay in the realm of the ego and the intellect is a great temptation because they are the natural products of concentration on the physical level, yet if the physical level is to be transformed, the ego, (as the tool of Will) and intellect, (as the tool of Intuition) must be ruled, governed and constantly directed by their higher aspects or correspondences of the Self.

When the light of the soul is lit within the personality, that personality must thereafter be brought more and more within the direction (Will) of the soul. From thence, when personality is not functioning under the soul's direction but continuing its own politics and games, there is much disharmony felt and the individual experiences the struggles known as 'discipleship'. Dissolving these blockages caused by the undisciplined personality becomes a major focus of the disciple's path, but little by little is control gained and primitive aspects of the personality can be utilised and trained for use by the soul.

How, one might ask, if the personality is the extension of the soul in the physical plane, can one be said to be distinct and out of synchronicity with the other? Just as in the early stages of evolution on the physical plane it was necessary for man to master the workings of the physical body until its function moment to moment became autonomous, so the mastering of personality is an evolutionary stage, which will one day be seen as primitive and far off to the advanced human on the physical plane.

Just as the human body is the mediator between the lower, basic form of matter and its higher equivalent of organised aggregations functioning autonomously—a stage between the elemental and the greater, more advanced form—so the personality is a stage between the lower, apparently non-physical attributes of will, love and active intelligence, (purpose, attraction and action) and the higher counterparts or expression of these aspects of God.

It is this mastery that mankind is learning. It is not a test, but a skill to be acquired, and while we talk of the body and personality as if they are separate, they are of course both expressions of the One force.

As humanity advances and the emotional needs of the personality are subsumed under the Will and mastery of the soul, greater and greater will shine the Light of spiritual peace upon the Earth. While individuals may appear to fall, step by step will this process be accomplished by all, until the remnants of the distant past are gone, atrophied by their own obsolescence, outnumbered by the higher forms. This process cannot be hastened except by the individual's effort to submit to the higher Will of their soul. The only danger lies in the mistaking of power games of the personality for a desired advancement of the soul. Only honesty in self-examination will reveal by which agency your life is steered.

Patterns, nurtured and repeated by the personality, stick to it like glue. In fact they are the stuff of which the personality is made, with which its life is imbued. That is why these patterns are so difficult to rent and dispel. To try to alter or discard patterns of the personality without the total reliance on and help of the soul is like taking a supporting wall from a house—the air may for a moment be able to whistle in, but very quickly the roof will fall down! Seek first the support of the soul. Once gained, communication with your soul renders you independent of the paths of others and brings, rightfully, your own true expression of being into the world. And once mastery of personality by soul is gained then that which is even higher can be looked for and attained.

When you feel attacked you have strayed from knowing who you are. You cannot feel powerless unless the power which is rightfully yours has been given away. In fact it can never be 'given away' any more than your life itself can be given away. You remain what you have always been, a continuous extension of God itself. Here in the physical world, at the outermost extreme of that extension you lose consciousness of the rest of yourself, but it never truly disappears except to retract into God itself in which case, how can you think that its power is then diminished?

When you withdraw permanently from your body and personality, of course they cease to be, but the rest of you, extended still as a wave, a thread of God, still is. Of course you are immortal! How could you not be? But your immortality requires not your 'death' to prove it. Is the caterpillar dead when it becomes a butterfly or is it simply the pupa which can be said to die?

Attend, with all your consciousness only to this moment and you will discover your immortality for in this moment you will find that there are no other moments and eternity is not a far-off dream but with you now. And when your brain, that restless personality of you, ceases to rush 'ahead' to be where it can never truly be, you find Life stayed behind to greet you. Journey into this moment and you will find it the only one there is, you will meet yourself there and God there, and find that you and God and the moment are One, and what seemed to be time was the fanciful notion of a flighty brain racing thither and yon upon its own inventions, swapping Life for anticipation, mistaking 'effects' for their cause and turning Truth into lies.

The 'mind' of the personality wanders everywhere trying to find gratification for its wants. Its needs arise from its sense of separation, the ultimate price of the journey of individuation. But you forget that the journey is simply an experiment in experience, not a Truth. Just as a well-made movie will convince your emotions, evoking fear or joy, ecstasy or loathing in you, so has this journey convinced the personality that it is not imagination but the Truth. Do you not see then why clinging to the personality cannot bring you to the Truth? The personality itself is a product of the journey and without the imagination of the journey it has no truth. Of course that is why the world seems scary and dangerous to you, because it is *not* the Reality of Truth!

When you see an old silent movie the characters flicker about the screen absorbed in their drama, which seems now to you more comedy then drama, so will the world seem to you when you leave behind its dreams and look upon it from the dispassion and 'distance' of the soul. Then and only then can real Love be felt and the matter of Earth raised by the spirituality of those who *know* themselves as souls, whose personalities no longer have control, and whose 'imagination' is used to enlighten Earth to heaven.

Relax your grip and Life will flow through the river of your veins. Try to control it and Life will seep through your closed fist like water. Against it you are nothing. Recognise it is all you really are. Think that Life is circumstance and you have not seen it at all. Hear it behind the sound of the ocean and you will have heard its power. Feel its light behind the dawn and you will have seen its glory. Recognise it in an act of kindness and you will have known its Love.

Take time to remove yourself from time to discover that the moment is forever. Let all else fall away in presence of this Truth and neither night nor day shall weary you nor shifting movement of the outer mind distract you. Heaven will be not a place of promise but a knowledge that lives inside you. Then will you know you go in peace but never leave Me, change or grow but stay just as you truly are.

So difficult the time you have between the worlds of soul and personality, the first awaiting the other clinging, pulling as hyenas fight to gain a bone. You long to return to what you think is 'home' yet 'home' is simply the elevated, elusive you. Seek no place, no building, no ritual, no thing, to bring this 'home' to you. It does not reside in these outer things. Inside, beyond the personality of you is home, and these internal doors may take you in but they also lead you out. Through them is the Light of God and worlds beyond imagining where you may travel without appearing 'lost' for having found yourself you are already home.

Will

How can a fearful heart return you joy? How can anxious mind bring you peace? Your freedom to choose is bounded by the Laws of cause and effect. You are one of a Whole, free to initiate the thought and action that creates a path, but it is the quality of the thought that determines the direction of the path. Those who sit in spirit watching you cannot rescue you from your chosen path. None is truly free to counter the free will of another. But your path with its direction will change the instant you truly change the quality of mind that fixes you upon track or way.

Action follows thought; not thought that flickers, floating, across the brain in scattered pieces a thousand times a day, but thought which is centred deep inside you. It is that which lies beneath the colour of your words—the fears, the open joys—that sit behind the outward pretence of you.

So, if you would know whence comes the quality of being back to you, examine honestly the contents of your heart, the alignment of your heart and thought and feeling of you. For all that heaven is, all that it can only be, is change of mind. It is not place or time or a just dessert for piety. It is a state instantly available at any 'time'. It requires not that you 'do' but that you *be* different and you can only *be* different in the quality of your heart-mind. It is the thought-feeling of you that gives rise to the actions of your life and only ruthless honesty shows exactly what qualities your thought-feelings are.

The traps of delusion are multitudinous. There is one for every attempt to separate your mind from God, the part from what it is as part of whole, the beingness of you from the beingness of others. Delusions come in many forms, each an attraction sought after by the 'independent' will of man. Discernment is the hard won skill of spiritually evolving man to know what comes from God and what is just a whim, a crude and glamorous desire of man. Crude indeed will seem the dishonesties of man when the light of honesty is shone upon them. Like a dark and sticky web they will seem, a sick joke blown away, their attractions disappear, and Wisdom, Truth and Power stand instead, revealed.

If you want your works to be effective in the world, they must have not only Love, which is only one attribute of divinity but also power (Will) and the active Intelligence of God. Love, truly felt, has activity, but because at the level of Truth it is inseparable from Will, it could be said that the activity of Love is driven by Will. In words only can these divisions be made.

Will, for your purposes of understanding, can be said to be essentiality of being. To bring something into being there must be Will. Your creations must have Love, but if they do not have the power of Will driving them, they remain in the weak and useless domain (spiritually speaking) of the glamorous, egotistical, desire nature of humankind. They cannot then serve. Truly, Love is not afraid of power. It is not afraid to see the destruction of that which is false and the small personality aggrandisements of man are false indeed.

Will is focused as the lazer beam. It does not set out to destroy but to be Truthful. It does not hide in the shadows but blazes forth its Light, cutting through the dross of emotionality.

Unless the noble intent of Love is driven by the forward motion arising from Will, it remains only an intent, a determinant of quality but not a guarantee of accomplishment into being. Similarly, without the quality of Love, Will serves only the little will of the personality and what is 'accomplished' does not serve the whole at all. Create therefore with Love, drive the creation with Will to bring it into being, and apply it with active Intelligence to ensure its right use in the realms of humanity.

Without Love, will becomes ideology, which must in the end be destructive, for without Love, will cannot be intelligently applied. From this lack both politics and business suffer in your world and the consequences are great for both planet and mankind. Love without Will is powerless intention, weakness giving in to apparent strength, but Love harnessed to Will would transform your politics and business and miracles be performed on Earth, for active Intelligence—the right application of Love and Will—is the daughter and son of the parents and follows automatically as consequence.

Meditation is the dedication of the mind to the discovery of Truth, but discovery of Truth is not confined to this method alone. Understanding and accepting your true Will, will spontaneously bring you discovery of Truth as you proceed actively through your day. Since each of you is an expression of Me, the true nature of your Will is likewise an expression of Me. This is why the right action of Will does not and cannot harm another since I do not attack Myself. Truth, being all there is, does not destroy itself.

Will is the driving force of your being. When your true Will—which has come directly from Me as the essential part of your constitution of mind, body and spirit—is denied, blocked, subverted to the control of others or in any otherwise distorted, its energy does not disappear but is imprisoned in the body to cause pain, illness and openness to disease. It must, because the body, your physicality, was the destination of its expression on this plane. You act with or through your body. The ultimate expression of Will is action.

Peeled of its layers of appearance therefore, all malfunction of the body can be discovered as a distortion of the Will force. Since Love and Will are inseparable for right action, then the feeling of the body and therefore the life on the Earth plane must include both. You cannot free suppressed Will within yourself without Love of that aspect of you which has been suppressed, and you cannot truly heal yourself if the 'process' of your healing is assumed to include the blame and punishment of those seen as oppressors of your will. True healing harms no one, even the bitterest of your former 'foes' unless they choose to perceive your healing as undesirable, in which case they are not in fact affected by your healing but by their own lack of Love for you.

To see your enemy healed of his hate must give you great cause for rejoicing. Each being freed from his own bonds raises the health of all for he no longer adds to the distortions prevalent in the world but clears them about himself, and others—coming into his field—meet not clouds of darkness, but the joy of Light and the pleasant company of a realised soul.

Right Will has no need to break or bend. It stands apart from the oppositions of the world. It does not partake of argument on form or 'right' but takes the view of honesty, that the motive of all concerned may be seen for what it is, that outcome be brought in line with soul intent, not personal 'political' gain.

That which you have called 'ego' is in its negative sense distorted Will. It is will that is not aligned with the higher Will of soul as an expression of God. Distorted by lifetimes of suppression, wrong expression and reaction to perceived limitation, it wrecks havoc on Earth because it is force wrongly directed. Ego or 'personality' on the Earth plane is, in its right understanding, the individual expression of God as you. It is not evil nor wrong but as necessary at this level of manifestation as is your body. The only 'wrong' involved has been its non-alignment with soul intent, with the truth of your unique expression of God that you are.

Just as the desert and the lush forest do not occupy the same space at the same time, it is not necessary that your personality and that of another be totally compatible at the same place and time. It is necessary, however, that you each retain and respect the uniqueness of yourselves and each other, recognising that God is the nature behind those divergent appearances. Do not give up your uniqueness on the Earth plane because it does not seem compatible with another personality form. That is suppression and leads to illness and imbalance, not only of yourself but of the human 'family' as well. In striving to embrace Love as the teacher of humankind you have denied Will, without which you have no being with which to know and express Love.

Because it is your vehicle for expression of Will in the world, your body registers both the right expression of Will and its suppression, denial or distortion. You call these reactions 'emotions' because you 'feel' them, they register somewhere within the body. Truly, Love and joy are pure expressions of God—your soul and spirit—and also register in the body. Can you not see then how health-giving these are to your physical being? Laughter that comes from joy can ripple out to others, its purity of sound raising the vibration of its surroundings, more potent than any concoction of man to heal the body or divert the course of the world.

The action of Will in the universe is seen as fire. It cuts through all that is not required on any plane, which is why it is said to purify. The fire of Will then can be said to be the agent of change. It rallies and moves the substance of being to carry out its intent. The still acquiescence of being, which is seen in substance as water, is 'opposed' or better said 'complemented' by the fire of Will.

It is the apparent division of God into Love and Will that produces the *apparent* duality of being so polarised in your world, for your world is, as it were, the farthest extent (as materialism must be) of this apparent movement in the substance of being.

From this apparent polarisation, all movement of God is 'produced,' the activity of Intelligence. What you see as the destructive nature of Will cannot be without Love, for without one truly the other is not, but is simply an imitation thereof. It is only from the human perspective that true Will must appear destructive for it is attachment to form that produces sense or feeling of loss. Without Will, Love has no intent and without Love, Will has no reason or purpose.

The action of Will is through fire, of which the flames of your known fire are but an echo and a physical manifestation of higher intent. To burn in the esoteric sense, is to purify, to turn what is no longer required back into the 'raw material' of being. Since fire is the active aspect of being, it is that which creates in the sense in which you know creation to be. Remember though, it does not create without the substance of Love—the apparently acquiescent aspect of being—for the two are one in the uncreated Stillness of potential being.

From your perception you give them many names; yin and yang, masculine and feminine, fire and water. Do you see then that to see one without the other is false and ineffectual. You cannot *experience* wholeness without recognition of both aspects of what is whole and so much of your social and political turmoil is produced by an inability to grasp the necessity and complementarity of these apparently dual aspects. Only when they become as one do you move beyond the petty and political and the ego-centric polarised central self of the personality you thought was you, and into the realm of real work and embrasure of Truth in the united soul of you.

Purification is the discarding of that which is false. Burning as purification in the esoteric sense is the destruction of the etheric structure built up by patterns of thought. This requires that you recognise that which is false. It is in the recognition of falsity and the decision to give it credence no longer that purification occurs. The essential, untainted, undistorted child within you shows you what is truly you and therefore enables the false to be distinguished from the Truth. None but you can stop the building of these walls that hide the Truth of you.

At all levels the purifying flame works for you. Punishment and burning by flame in the physical world is a distortion by man, with no real understanding of the true purity of flame. 'Purification' by fire without Love is not purification at all but an attempt to transfer what needs to be purified in oneself, (from a higher plane) onto others in the physical plane. The result is ego masquerading as Love for Love never harms in the real sense and Will does not suppose its own path to be another's.

Those who burned the 'witches' sought to purify themselves but bearing not to see the fault inside, cast it out upon others. Honesty creates its own flame, burning off the substance of self-deception. Remember, even the apparent love humanity extends can be deceptive, clinging to its own desire, its 'honesty' twisted for attention or personal gain. To try to purify one's soul by physical fire is to misunderstand completely the laws of cause and effect. True purification comes always from the plane of higher intent.

You have not advanced enough yet, you race called 'men,' to know which fires of the physical realm are a result of Earth purging the old aspects of herself that space may be made for the flowering of her new and higher intent. The fires that purify the soul have no heat in the physical sense. Love, with its consort Will, burns through what is false. It sees past social games and dishonest intent. It judges not those caught in their games of astral confusion, of emotional gratification, but dispels them as if they were never there, which to the clear Light of Love's bright flame, they are not.

Once lit, the flame dies never, flaming through the times of doubt, burning bright on waters calm for other travellers' way to shine. When the human side of you bogs your feet in sticky glue, burn bright the flames and enter in. Purify and cleanse the limbs upon which hangs the carcass of your greater sin, the rank denial of divinity, the lack of knowing who you are and who it is that dwells within.

Cast no one out from the net of your love but gather all into your heart that you too might find a place there. The cost of being human is too great sometimes and you must free yourself before the burden of the human way crushes out the name of God that links you to the very soul of you that lights the flame that is your fuel, that drives you on and burns away the murky dross with brilliant flame.

Those aspects of the personality which seem hard to let go are easily burned off by connection to the soul's intent. Their shedding is automatic for they cannot exist in the higher planes of soul intent. You see then, that when your personality is taken over by the higher intent, you automatically cease to add to the emotional fog and misplaced loves of the world, and with practise of staying your life in this state of higher intent you destroy the residue of these grey clouds of murky ego purpose, and help those about you by the clarity of your own intent.

Clarity of soul intent is not fanaticism, which is simply the small will of man unaligned to the Light and sensitivity of Love's higher sight. Fanaticism always thinks itself right. Love, while not allowing injustice and dishonesty to prevail, leaves others to find Truth their own way. Love, married to Will, does not punish nor hate but shows the way. It is not weak and is unshakeable in the face of 'danger,' for it knows Truth to be Reality and the physical to be merely echoes. It sees Life where the ignorant see death and its hand is always steady for it knows not weakness nor death.

Nothing can be said of the true nature of man which cannot also be said of the nature of God. Since man is made of the substance of God, the attributes of God must be available to man. God is free to create as He will, so it is with man. What to man is a deep mystery is to God a passing experiment fleeter than the flight of gnats yet frozen in eternity, for in the consciousness of God there is no time. Whatever man attends to exists at the moment for him. Herein lies the *action* of free will.

Your emotions cling around your finer being. They make a sticky glue inhibiting your movement, clouding your judgement and hiding the way. Fear is ever the basis of emotion not founded in divine Love. Truly, Love cannot have fear because it sees honestly. It does not string itself to the agendas of others for it stands in its own power, clear of such games. It is not hurt and does not doubt itself according to the shifting attractions of others, because it sees that which is false, that which is relative and dependent on perception and circumstance.

Such Love cannot be found outside of you, for this outside is a whirling debris of scattered thought and unharnessed power, a maelstrom of self-indulgence and denial of what is greater than that which the personality desires. The inside, unchanging God in you has Love—unswerving, unchanging, complete unto itself as God is complete. Aligned with Will it is unaffected by the apparent 'power' of others. In application it must be wise for Intelligence is its child. It is not filtered through any screens of social nicety, no matter how well dressed they may be to appear as compassion or sympathy. Too often these are not, but simply petty power disguised through lack of honesty. The children of God are honest. How can they be otherwise?

You allow others to control you when you don't trust yourself. When you trust your own judgement on what is right for you, you are empowered by that trust and can stand free of attempted oppression of your will. Your little will, in the end, brings only confusion and antagonism, and when you have at last done with these, then submit your tiny will to the greater Will. The rocks hurled by the rampant games of man will pass you by, glancing past you as they fly. You cannot feel them, shielded by the greater Will within. The greater Will is not sought as protection. You find it not, if protection is what you seek.

Truth & Faith

In the vastness of being, the door to evil is so small, yet as human beings you are so attracted to this tiny part of possibility. As long as you recognise evil you cannot meet it by running away. It is part of your mind and until it is expelled from your mind it must exist in and for you. Fight not evil with more fear for fear is the basis of evil. Replace it instead with Truth. The cutting edge of Truth is so bright and hard nothing can stand against it for that which is 'against' Truth *is* nothing. So fear not, children of the Light, but go forth to Truth—not with the weakness of arrogance but with the power of humility—and Truth shall light the way for you as surely as sunlight creates the day.

And what is this Truth? That all in the world beside you are part of you, that what you are may help or hinder them, for as you believe together so is your reality one. As you raise yourself in consciousness you lighten the way for others, dispelling with your clarity the fogs with which you surround each other. The fogs are emotional; clouds of doubt and fear and negativity, ignorance of karmic Laws, superstition and fantasy. Fantasy is the small desire of man, seeing that which is not there, constructing games of petty power, an assumption, a hope of personal gain.

In the end, personal gain is nothing at all, it dissolves, as fantasy is want to do, and only Truth remains. It is not fantasy to know the other forces in the world with you, the creatures of the natural world, as much an expression of God as you, and in the child-like 'imagination' of the open soul is much revealed that humankind hitherto has thought was 'fantasy'. No, the fantasy of which we speak is the tangled web of emotive games your tiny self weaves for you: games of social 'grace' or political gain; useless games which do not place the whole before the tiny one. Human 'love' it is often assumed, always has noble intent, yet it is a glamour that hides not nobility but manipulative intent and through it the web of human suffering extends, not just through a tyrant's hand but through the stranglehold and control of social 'love'.

Honesty begins with Self. When honesty of Self governs the personality a freedom comes, for honesty is the truth of you allowed to *be*. Honesty leads to right judgement, right judgement to right action. It is not seduced by the glamorous webs of social interaction, will not shy from picking up a fallen brother and setting him upon his way.

It will not be fooled by the games people play, will hold silence when others might speak and speak when the opportunity for correction of error comes its way. Error may be a lack of honesty or ignorance of the lighted way. Compassion tells honesty when to speak and what to say.

Honesty will never lie, it is an open lotus flower in which a certain kind of darkness cannot bide. Delusion is a form of darkness, the tricks you play upon yourself. The delusion of mankind is a murk so deep it puts a band of smoke about the Earth so thick the angels barely find their way. But every time a human opens up their flower of Truth and looks with honest heart upon themselves, a shaft is cleared, a way is found, and Light upon the human ground pours down and there upon the Earth is found the shining clarity of heaven.

Honesty *is* clarity. It is not clouded by social convention nor manipulated by personal desire, for then it is not honesty at all but 'justified' opinion. Honesty is never critical, it simply tells the truth. It cuts through correctness and joins you as sister and brother. The true heart speaks clearly to the mind. It guides the conscience and stops political ambition holding sway.

The Will of God cannot be dishonest. It blazes forth in greater brightness than the day. It recognises no impediment, for what can impede that which sits behind all movement, and joined with Love rolls unstoppable, being the only real 'action' there is. Honesty is a quality of being. Honest being is not disappointed by the lies that surround it for it knows that other people's self-deception does not alter the Truth of who they really are. How can a sham, a pretence to be what one is not, alter what one truly is? But the honest son of God will hold a mirror to his brother's lies.

Dishonesty produces chaos. It clouds the mind and blocks the path. It turns a son of God into a worm upon the ground. Peace held together with lies is not peace at all but weary truce and before long, personalities, disappointed, do battle again for supremacy to satisfy the lack they feel inside. Honesty, like humility, is a quality of strength. It is born of Will where humility is born of Love. Each follows from its parent as surely as right action follows from the Intelligence of Love and Will combined.

Truth is that which changes not. It is beyond apparent reason and is not relative nor dependent on view or circumstance. Yet your view of it will change as your perception moves from the egocentric view of man to the wider view of soul, which includes not only man but those other expressions of Creation that sit in being beside you.

It can be said that at every level there is truth peculiar to that level. It can also be said these truths are facts, not Truth. They simply are the way things are. The seeker seeks the Truth that changes never. The word from which all other words come forth. Not a sound as you perceive it though it has its echo in what you know as sound. The word of Truth *is* in

Stillness and fullness. It sits undivided behind all that appears at any level to be. Truth is not for comprehension but for knowing, beyond understanding yet it brings understanding, not of itself, (because it is both the cause and fullness of itself) but of its effects. Once something in form is seen as an effect and not a cause its power disappears, and you as consciousness yourself do not give *your* power to these effects.

Beyond Truth there is nowhere to go, and from it all springs forth, for it *is* all that can possibly be, and once realised, you have begun the journey back to what you already are in truth, pure uncreated potential. You have turned from fascination of the journey to contemplation of the potential 'to be'. Concentration into form is but one way to explore this potential 'to be'. And there are other ways and other planes in which to move.

One who works at a higher level, who disciplines himself not to fall prey to form and effect is a master for he or she has ceased to attend solely to effects and pays all attention instead to the plane of intent. Intent, we must repeat, is a quality of soul. It is only consciousness not form which can have intent. The personality thinks it has intent but it is loose, undisciplined and solely self-referential, no matter how 'well-intentioned' it may appear to be. Personality directed by the soul must have a higher intent. It is not fooled by personal desire, its own or any other's. Discernment comes from revelation, a glimpse of what is soul and what is personality 'you'. Discretion follows naturally and what is real integrity is simply soul intent.

The higher planes of being are calm and subtle. To the unaccustomed inner eye it may seem that nothing is happening there. The closer one gets to the centrality of being, the more still it must appear to be, since the divine source is Still and moves not.

Faith is a state of being oft misunderstood by you. True or 'correct' faith correctly applied, is the inevitable outcome of knowledge. It is not founded in blind prediction according to man's desire for what it is he puts his faith in, but on knowledge of the level of cause above the plane in which he desires effect. Even so, it is not the physical detail of outcome that the faithful can expect but the *quality* of effect. The higher up your chain of command you place your desire—whereon you place your faith—the more appropriate will be the quality of the effect for that which is truly desired.

Desire and faith are both the key and the door that your key will unlock. If desire is bound by the personality, (which answers only to its tiny self) that cluster of feelings of wants and ambitions is the arena of desire for you, and the rewards returned will be as transitory as the personality itself and the world of physical effects in which it dwells. The desire or better put, the aspiration of the soul, looks far beyond personal gain and raises that which was purely personal to a greater gain—a larger term view beyond the small and finite 'self'. Its quality is that of aspiration to a higher good, to a plane unseen by the lower you. That's why the faith required by the personality in the level of the soul, is 'blind,' for it is not the personality but the soul that has eyes to walk you unhindered in the planes of the soul.

The outcome of faith in the qualities of the soul may or may not be seen on Earth, and often even if they can be 'seen' they are not recognised as effects at all, but chance or luck or circumstance that carry with them an inexpressible lifting of heart-mind to joy and Love pervading, joy and Love often excruciating in their intensity. Though these moments are fleeting, they leave an indelible mark on the memory and a longing for return to these qualities of soul.

In the planes of the soul a wider Light links the 'individual' soul to other souls. Separation is not concretised and none exists truly apart, but each move and in freedom, meld with one another. Yet individuation, as you understand it, is still a hallmark of that plane.

When the human has contact with his soul he can operate more consciously (from the personal point of view) upon this Earthly plane. He begins to understand the relationship of quality to cause and how effects are made. The danger here for human kind is that the astral buzz of human desire clouds the pure judgement of the mind and faith wavers or is placed back and forth between the lower and the higher planes, squandering intent and selling short effect.

Faith then, you may perhaps now understand, is simply attention, and to whatever you give your attention, the quality of that intention, which is inextricable from the quality of that which is attended to, must determine the effects that come to you. When faith or attention remain in the levels of the soul, greater will be the reward to you, and the personality—at last subsumed by the higher being of you—ceases to clamour its own attention and the 'faith' of soul fills the life of the personality with the Light of the soul.

'Having faith' simply means that the specific outcomes of the physical world are set in operation on the level of the soul. It means that the 'outcome' must be for a greater good since the soul plane is a plane of non-separation and what is accomplished there must be felt by these non-separated 'units' or souls.

Any 'faith' that effects an outcome on Earth which advantages one over another, thus placing a greater barrier of separation between them, is not faith of the soul at all, but the desire of the personality to separate and control for gratification and power of its own tiny ends. There is no merit therefore in such personal gain and in no way can such 'merit' store up 'points' for one in 'heaven'. Your consciousness is either in heaven (which you define at present as the home of the soul) or it is not. The consciousness expresses 'heaven' or 'hell' of its own making, the keys for which are yours, provided by the function of free will.

Do you have faith that two and two are four? This requires no 'faith' for surely it is knowledge? You see, it is in the surety of knowledge that faith *is*. Move out of knowledge and the quality of faith becomes not faith but hope. Hope is based on desire and 'hopeful' expectation, and is therefore not faith (which is knowledge) at all. Beware then, that your blind faith is not faith at all but hope parading as knowledge. There is no certainty in hope but there is certainty in knowledge. Aim therefore, for knowledge, not inflexible belief, which is just hope set in rigidity, but true, spiritual knowledge which ever hovers beyond description, requiring a change of state to know it and requiring the Will to Good to bring it 'down,' to infuse the world with it.

Trust grows from knowledge. To *know* what something is, is to accept what it is, and to clearly know the quality of something is to have an appropriate trust in it. When you learn to discern truth from illusion you do not misplace your trust in the illusion. When you understand the level of cause, you do not put your trust in effects. This is the proper basis for prayer. Prayer is simply the right focus of attention. 'Prayer' in some form or other is what you do all the time because you are consciousness and whatever state your consciousness is in *is* your prayer because does not your state of consciousness bring effects?

If you place your trust in the billiard balls and not in the skill and intent of that which drives the cue, your trust is placed in something that cannot master its own action and such trust is no more than haphazard hope of luck. So much time and effort is wasted in your world by trust in such 'luck'. How much could be achieved by knowing the cause of effects, and by constant attention to the encouragement or elimination of consciousness that gives rise to certain effects. You punish the thief's behaviour but do not change the mind that caused it.

The constant stream of consciousness that is your life is your prayer. Effective prayer, prayer that *changes* for the higher good of all, is simply the raising of consciousness to the causal planes. To have the perfect outcome—in the spiritual sense—in the world of effects, one must trust, by right attention of consciousness, the perfection of higher intent.

To the personality such trust may seem at first blind since higher intent belongs to the planes not inhabited by the personality. But to place your trust in that plane is to submit to the knowledge of the soul, and later to its greater Self or Spirit, the unity of that which is above the soul. By this you create a clear channel for the effects flowing from that higher plane to spread down and out upon the Earth and its effects appear 'miraculous'. You have in fact 'raised Earth to heaven' for being of a quality of the spiritual planes, that's what a miracle is, a pathway in the consciousness of heaven. Miracles are not partisan. They benefit all since they operate on the level of unity. Small or selfish intent cannot bring a miracle though it may bring about, temporarily at least, the desired effect. As it began on the plane of temporality, its effects will only be on that plane.

A miracle recognises the eternity of unity, thus its 'reverberations' go on forever since unity recognises only the ever-present. Ponder on this and you will see how very different are the realities of different planes of consciousness. When your consciousness is limited to the material plane of reality you are trapped in its effects. Yet this entrapment is a choice not a necessity, neither is it a 'sentence' for an inherent fault in your being. It is simply a choice of all those who operate in the consciousness of the personality, and you are no more required to stay in that reality than you are to stay in the imaginative reality of a movie once the reel is played and the movie is over.

Have no fear of God. If you have any fear at all of God you have not understood what God is. When you understand that God is nearer to you than your very breath, you have glimpsed what God is. When Love has replaced your judge-ment of yourself, you have glimpsed what God is. When all your darkness is lit by His Loving acceptance of you, you have begun to experience what God is.

Let the closeness of God be in your awareness, in every moment and you will have no need. Abundance comes from knowing His nearness since as He *is* abundance, abundance must be yours in the knowing of Him. It is not a concept, far off, to be called upon when you think you lack, but a state in which you exist, for abundance is God which is Life itself, and how in this can there be lack? To feel God nearer than your hands and feet, closer than your head and wrapped deep inside your heart, is to live in truth and safety, to never be without, and that which seemed outside of you becomes transformed as you view it from within.

So if you would live with freedom in the world, one of the ingredients of your life must be faith, certainty of the reality that you exist in other planes. Learn to move between them that the consciousness of Earth be raised to heaven, for how can it not be so if the consciousness of all remain in heaven? Earth too is consciousness, greater than all you have dreamed to comprehend, and so truly can Earth reside in heaven, and then beyond, in other heavens where still greater beings reside, their consciousness so vast the universe does not contain them, and the multitude of stars just sprinkled pollen dust drifting from the flowers in the garden of their thought.

Structure & Form

All thought gives rise to structure and form. Thought is an energy, thus it has the power to move the lesser aspect, matter, on your plane. What happens on the physical plane holds true on the other planes. The 'reality' of each plane is determined by the 'thought' that governs it. The quality of thought in fact *is* the plane. This is why your thought raises you to heaven or creates a very hell for you. How could it be other-wise in the Oneness which God is?

As human beings, you judge something by appearance, which is its effect, not its cause. Can you not see then why, if you would progress, if you would create a heaven of your life on Earth, you have no option but to attend to the quality of your thought?

All that is sent forth from the source of thought has shape. Because you live in a three-dimensional world you think of shape that way. The further a thing is from the source of its being the more it is bounded, in your terms the more shape it has. Does colour have shape? Yes, but it is not such as you would recognise it, being a quality behind, not of, the physical plane.

Shape has property just as colour has property. When you immerse yourself in a colour on the inner planes you know in its totality all that it contains. A shape also is the information of itself. So it is that in the great scheme of Creation, the Lords of Karma, who are also Lords of Form, have devised the shapes that enable the energy of thought to build, in manifested form, the outcome of thought. One of these, the triangular shape is of particular importance in the shaping of your world, your life and the lives of all the beings who journey with you today.

Triangularity is a quality of universal mind different from spherality. Triangles express being in different ways to spheres. They are different aspects of being and therefore function in different ways. Like the sphere, the triangle is perfectly balanced, but in its own way. Each part of it supports the other parts.

The triangle transmits. Its lines continue beyond the intersection of its points. Thus whatever intention the triangle has is transmitted on the inner planes in the multitudinous directions of its planes. The triangle then can be said to be communication, amongst other things. The triangle also speaks of order. Like a crystal, its parts are built rank upon rank allowing the clear transmission of a message. Like a   crystal, the triangle will receive and amplify your thought. This is part of the key to understanding this age of the planets that make up your world. Though all things might be at bottom spheres, coming into or ceasing to be, they are arranged, these component spheres into the shape appropriate for the evolution and order of the plane in which they appear to be.

Love, Will and active Intelligence are the ingredients of structure and form. They are the creative triangularity of your world, of your solar system at its present time, each supporting the other in a creative, dynamic wholeness. The triangle then also symbolises creation in the active sense whereas the sphere represents the completeness of that which gave rise to Creation. All things coming into creation radiate, it is true. The action of involution need not concern you.

Look carefully at what you say. You will see that the words you use have shape. They are as much a form impacting on the world as are the winds and rain. When Will and Power are placed behind your words they focus the energy of the thought that formed them. The world of modern man is full of words, the majority emotion-bound as it is emotion that forms them.

As we have said the emotions of man are invented in imitation of the great emotion of God, Love. But these emotions are at best imitations, at worst attempts at opposition to the emotion of God and thereby useless in benefiting you beyond the small desires that sent them forth. Can you see then how most of the words cramming up the spaces of the world are too a mindless imitation at best and at worst a mockery of Good? Your words come from your thought. They build your life for you and bombard others with effects as surely as arrows pierce the skin. Before you speak ask where your words are coming from and feel the quality of what you wish to say, and ask yourself if indeed these words should be loosed upon the world.

Structure is the result of energy organised into patterns. It is the result, manifestly, of qualities of energy. Different worlds, even different universes are the result or expression of large categories of qualities of energy. Perception of one part of Creation by another occurs only when the quality of energy of each is sufficiently compatible. How could it be otherwise, since perception is itself a patterning or organisation of energy? Think on this well and you will discover much—that perception creates the limits of your life, locking the perceiver into experience of particular energies. So, if you would have the experience of a master, you must see as a master sees.

Life is not limited to the structure and form known on Earth. Even on other planets within the physical universe there are patterns and structures of different forms which man will never see while the quality of pattern of his own perception is limited.

Structure and form can also be said to be organisations of consciousness. A change of *your* consciousness therefore, will bring you a vastly different view, for you will have moved into another strata of patterning, a different quality of energy, a different band of experience, and thus a whole new world, opens up for you. Can you see then, that you must *be* what it is you desire? You must move into that band of consciousness in which that which you desire *is*. This holds for every level of manifestation and thus it is that poverty begets poverty and wealth, wealth. And if you would have wealth of the spirit, your consciousness must be that of Spirit.

The small movements of your world, the myriad manifestations of your planet's life, are governed by the larger patterns of consciousness through which the Logoi of your Earth, planets and sun are passing. Thus your planets too have times of change, growth and rebirth, and their bodies may be left behind or transmuted as the consciousness indwelling them transcends.

Structure both expresses an energy and enables an energy to express. Always, the key is both the visible shape you see and the complementary shape it leaves behind. Squares, triangles, spheres are fundamental energy patterns that govern the larger movements and directions of your universe of form. The movement is 'physical,' the 'direction' esoteric, for whatever has structure or form has a higher correspondence to which the form is simply a response. Although all are waves of Light emanating from the One, those waves create patterns and while outwardly squares, triangles and circles may seem to form, each, behind the grossness of this patterning, are waves.

Much has been said about the illusion of form. Illusion lies in the assumption that Life begins and ends in form. To know the illusion of form is not to deny it, but to have governance over it, not to exploit nor to master it in others, but in your own manifestation of it in you. True mastery does not attempt to alter another form of God's expression but to understand and realise what it is. When you recognise and deal with the energy behind a given form, that form must alter according to any alteration of the will behind it. This mankind has understood only in a primitive way, thinking that to master is to control and destroy that which is perceived to 'stand in one's way'. In this you have dealt only with the twisted emotional energy of the personality not aligned to the higher intent of the soul. The energy you have dealt with has not been the pure energy of higher intent, therefore the effects wrought by your control have not healed nor harmonised, but created havoc in the world.

You bring rightness into your relationship with form when you align the higher nature of your Love and Will, and then, as will be clear from your ponderings of these offerings here, right action automatically must follow, and form—the densest substance of being—is altered according to this correctly aligned action of Will.

The structure of anything in the physical universe is governed by the quality of the intent that sent it forth and intent is an attribute of consciousness. From the measured orbit of planets to the building of man's edifices, this is so. Intent is the *organising* attribute of consciousness. You cannot separate intent and consciousness any more than wetness and water can be separated. The intent aspect of consciousness marshals universal substance and even though elsewhere we have said that the devic realms are the form builders of your world, they are still responding as agents of that quality of intent determined by consciousness, be it your consciousness or that of a mighty cosmic being or master. The difference between an ordinary man and a master is that the master has taken control of his intent.

God is like a big soup of *all* potentiality. Yet this potentiality occupies neither time nor space, both of which are products, illusions if you like, of that potential. This is why you are exhorted to seek the Stillness of God, for in this Stillness lies the potential for your mastery of all that comes forth from that potential.

The magic of being is that you need not know *how* to construct the waveforms, the patterns, that create the structures of your life i.e. the forms or events that bring your intent back to you in manifestation. The quality of your intent automatically does that for you. It leads you to the appropriate learning, the people, the places, whatever it is that is needed. But remember, if you have handed your intent to your soul or to your higher Self, what transpires may not match what your personality thought to be the outcome of its desire.

Chaos and order are both structures emanating from consciousness. It is not possible for the personality to grasp always the cause or greater intent behind apparent chaos. There is a sense, paradoxically, that even in chaos there is order since it too is the result of intent, and manifestation follows in orderly pattern from the quality of intent. Do you see then how right prayer and the raising of man's consciousness to a level of high intent can alter outcomes, even when great forces are at work? For prayer is itself a quality of intent, and if practised in certainty, not hope, for the highest good, it must harness the mighty potential that God is.

Your being just *is,* but intent shapes the quality of your experience, accessing different aspects of that beingness depending on the quality of the intent. Mankind will advance with unprecedented speed when he grasps these facts about the quality of intent and applies right spiritual practise to the choice of his intent. Essential to that understanding is that all lie in the potentiality of God and to practise any form of so-called spirituality that sees one man or group as separated from the rest will not advance the cause of higher intent. How could it, when to move closer in consciousness to that which God is, is to move to greater and greater joinings, to be more and more aware of the Stillpoint in which all potential is contained, unseparated and at rest.

Never grieve the loss of that which is no longer useful. Measure usefulness with your soul, not your personality intent. Would you keep a broken china cup when the grail stands ahead of it all shone with holy Light? No, and so it should be with all that you materially hold dear, be it a decoration for your dwelling or a body that has served you well. How hard it is to see from where you stand, the shiny brightness of the greater plan! See beyond, bring that which is beyond into your now. The Light of the grail cup's already there if you would but drink of it!

When the world about you crumbles, and nothing seems to you as it was meant to seem, look again. What has gone has left an opportunity for something new. What will you place where grief and loss now stand? A monument? Or a shiny thing, built of Love, based not on grief but understanding? Does the butterfly stand and mourn the wrecked cocoon, bereft that it no longer crawls or does it dry its crumpled wings and fly?

Earth

Innocence is that part of you which comes to Earth untainted. It knows nothing of the limitations placed around it by man's definition of what he is. It is the pure essence of your Will. It lies in stillness beneath the armouries of doubt and fright built in fabrication to 'defend' itself against attack of brutality and ugliness, denial and non-acceptance, where it sought no more than self-expression. Its armouries may be brought again and again to each lifetime or they may be left behind that essence may arrive in innocence. Few are they who do not build a web of lies about their essence, yet underneath, the being that they are is always there for them to see.

Childlike it appears, for childhood should bear of no pretence, and when Earth is rid of all the lies of man, indeed the innocent of spirit will remain. So find beneath the layers of convention and conceit, the essence, yay the innocence of you, and take it with you through the trials of your day. Protect it not with pretence or it will scream at you to let it free. Let it tell you its abhorrence of the horrors that it sees that you might know the difference between innocence and forms of greed. For if all would stay and honour the Will of their essential being, rightness would return to Earth and innocence find on Earth a place to dwell.

Driven by angel speed now must be your blessing on the Earth. Many see what has been brought upon Her but act

not for fear of their own demise. But how can you protect
yourself from the consequence of Life? Such a little will it
takes to change a life and what could the addition of your
greater Will achieve? The beingness of you and the beingness of Earth cannot be separated as you seem to deem.
Your very manifestation here is built from Her. Not one
part of your bones did not grow from Her substance. Not
one breath your body takes that does not use Her own
product, air. You had a hand in Her creation it is true, but
how, you know not. It is better said to be co-creation and
you are bound to each other as closely as the water with the
sea. How can you not be since Earth and you are Me?

Behold Me as you go about your little day. What you
have tried to distance from yourself cannot in Truth be set
apart. The actions you pass on for another to amend must
return to you, in the end. You cannot take an action in the
day without affecting Me, cannot bless a plant or stone or
tree but you give thanks to Me.

Poet or businessman, mother, grass, flame or tree, all
are expressions of me. Can you not see then, all you do to
the Earth, you do to Me. And if you do it to Me you do it
also to yourself. So easy it is to take another path! So easy
to turn and say no, I will do this another way. So easy to
create sustainability instead of waste, to nurture instead of
plunder. It requires only the marriage of Love and Will.
How can your energy not affect the Earth which in its
physicality is also energy manifesting as form? Bless all that
live in the world with you. Bless them just because they
are, not just other human beings but all other creatures and
features of the Earth that share this place with you.

Acceptance of another's beingness is truly Love, for
acceptance judges not but allows the other to be. You
cannot rightly bless without acceptance. A 'blessing' that
is conditional upon your good judgement is not a blessing
at all but an imposition of your will upon another. Neither

does your blessing on another involve acceptance of the imposition of their will upon you.

Your body especially must be blessed. Repository of all your fears and woes, it suffers twice; first from what you place upon it and second from your complaint of it when that which you have placed on it manifests as hurt or pain to you. To bless the body is not to deny God, but to accept and Love the expression of God in the world, as your body is the instrument of this.

A blessing can be said to be the Loving acceptance of God in something, be it person, dog, cat, tree, land, stream or whatever. A blessing is not contingent upon the appearance or behaviour of that thing but upon recognition of its being-ness and joy at the diverse expression of what is. When you establish right acceptance, judgement ceases and you cease to attract and hold to yourself a state of imbalance. Relinquish-ment of judgement is not acquiescence to a state of affairs that is clearly against your Will. That also is imbalance.

There is much confusion about emotion. Once a feeling has occurred do not hold judgement against it but accept that it is. Then, if you are uncomfortable with the feeling, choose another way. Choose not because of a judgement against yourself or others for what has occurred, because judgement creates a bond that prevents a feeling from being released, and you become consciously or unconsciously chained to an emotion-response that may be unwanted or inappropriate. Held and denied emotion that is not truly desired is stored as etheric matter and because of the causal connection between the etheric 'body' and the physical body, adversely affects the physical body and pain and suffering result.

Those struggling to establish direction from their soul and higher Self have mistakenly judged against emotional response en masse, forgetting that human emotion is a reflection of Love. Love has been rightly described as the attraction principle, but it is only half of the apparent polarity that appears in the movement of My creation. I AM One and without Will, Love has no existence, as without Love, Will in truth has no existence. Peace comes to mankind when Love and Will are both accepted and understood and the distinctions of man disappear and argument about the nature and expression of Me cease for they are seen for what they are—false divisions born of the distance you have placed between your minds and Truth.

Although we have said that feelings (sentience) are an aspect of Will, and emotion an imitation of Love, this distinction is misleading for it invites the intellect to tread the paths of analysis and further increase its delve into divisiveness. Yet words on these pages are the only means by which these concepts can be presented at this time, and as with visual imagery, you must allow the understanding to come to you not through loud and literal recitation but through the stopping of semantic constraint and intellectual fence-building. Allow preconceived notions to disappear and new understanding arise from the totality of what is being presented to you here.

Judge not the form by which another chooses to gain his understanding. Accept that as his learning and do not impose your will on his teaching of himself. Do not either allow his teaching to impose itself on you unwelcome. To allow another to impose their will unwelcome upon you is to give your will to them. Harmlessness is the right use of Will in relation to others but it does not involve betrayal of your own Will.

Remember you are a unique expression of Me, and if you give your power to another you cannot then in that instant be expressing truly that aspect of Me which you are, and the energy which sent you forth as that expression is blocked. But it is still pouring forth and must be dealt with sooner or later, its flow allowed again to be. Emotion—the incorrect expression of Love—occurs because a build up of this energy has occurred. Emotion (in the human sense) is the result of mistreated, angered or blocked sentience and those whose rage spills out in violence against others do so in an attempt to save themselves from the 'danger' of releasing the flood gates of blocked anger, distorted and subverted by inappropriate use and unacceptance of the existence of the sentience of Being, and its expression, Will.

If you were manifesting with total freedom on the Earth plane, your form would change with your whim. In fact it does this at the subtler levels as your will and thereby your feelings, alter. Your body is currently rigidly limited by the boundaries you have placed about your understanding and as a consequence, your experience. There are many analogies we could use to demonstrate this, but let us for now take music as the lesson. A person with little understanding or mastery of an instrument can play only limited sound, the 'music' produced scarcely passing for music at all. But if that person acquires an understanding of the passion, the range of feelings, the beingness of a piece of music, which is greater far than the limits he previously placed upon the form, i.e. the instrument, he produces a melodious and evocative music that enables the instrument to truly be a vehicle that appears to totally transcend the limits of the instrument's form.

So it is with your body. When you understand the level of cause, when you embrace with the gladness and fullness of your heart, the passion, limitlessness and joy of Life as known by your Will, you can remove the limits to your Love and thus express in its fullness and limitless beauty the Life available to you, and the body seems to transcend the limits of form to express the greatest music of all.

Time is not applicable to the higher planes. It is as we have said, a function of the apparent distance of a waveform from its stillpoint at its source. The 'farther' a wave's distance from that stillpoint, the slower it becomes and slowness appears as density of solid form. The 'faster' a wave is, the 'lighter' it is, the less dense it must be, thus the less physical it appears to be and more rapid transformation is possible. The faster the waveform, the 'higher' its vibration.

Dense physicality on Earth, and its apparently long history, is produced by the tremendous length, and therefore slowness, of waveforms. Faster and slower waves can exist concurrently of course, hence life on Earth or in its surrounding field can be of myriad types from the physically dense to the ethereally misty, to the rapid, sparkling Light of angelic consciousness. You have the ability to fix your being, your awareness at any level, just as the musician can play according to his skill and understanding and desire, at any level of musicality. Your range of expression through the physicality of your body is even greater than that of the musician in our analogy because the elements that make up your physical form respond directly to your conscious command, arranging themselves according to your skill and direction, even as the sound energy from an instrument is arranged by the will and skill of the musician.

See you then how false it is to bind yourself by the constraints of time, as if time were truly a limit, a box to your consciousness, to your being? To look constantly to denser waves of the past is to travel only at one level of being and to give your power there when it could be going to great benefit of you and all to consciousness of higher levels that can impact directly on the instant, yet everlasting, present. Yet you drag yourselves around as if there were no other way of being, suffering enormously, and along with yourself, impose suffering on the planet and those who live here with you.

To be as you have always been in the past is to deny the possibilities of the present and to live not in Truth but in a false world of echoes. How good it feels to truly embrace the present! It frees your will to deal with now and in the instant of realisation of power of the present, fear automatically dissolves because fear, of its nature, is always based on the past. Even fear for the future must be based on experiences of the past. You cannot recover your lost power by attending to the long, slow waves of the past, echoing slowly and densely back and forth over the lighter planes of your world. But you can live truly in the present and cease to create at denser levels. When all understand the transforming power of the present, life on Earth will be transformed, not in the slowness of time but in the instant when the falsity of time is abandoned and enlightened consciousness becomes the action of those present.

You wish for abundance but deny you have fear of Me. Your fear binds you to that which you fear as surely as love binds you to that which you love. Accept that you have feared Me and your acceptance will turn fear instead into a bridge of rainbow light growing a flower of joy where there was denial. So, embrace all of your fears. Like erring children acknowledge their existence, not as punishment to wallow in but to know you have created them and accept them as part of yourself which they are. That which is denied cannot be transformed. Someone cannot take a gift you give them when their hands are tied, and denial of how you feel ties your hands that would otherwise accept abundance from Me.

Man has sought expansion of his industry in denial and imitation of the abundance of Me. But denial is the opposite of expansion, it compresses what should otherwise be free to grow and evolve, and in the name of false expansion you have laid waste the abundance of the Earth which I gave freely to thee. Denial blocks the Will and slows the vibration of thee, like a black hole densing and condensing what comes within its influence, as lightness and true expansion lightens joyfully all that touches them. You need not sit in heavy mediation on the problems of your world seeking to solve by further densification that which is dense enough already! By attending to the lightness of your being you automatically lighten the world.

What fears except those of grief are not lighted by Love and laughter? And grief is but a misunderstanding of Me. Accept that you have been, and are afraid, and wrongly thought you beheld the wrath of Me when truly you beheld only the consequence of thought. What is disaster is always evidence of denial. Accept your denials but criticise them not, for criticism itself is a denial of your truth and beauty, and let those who continue to fear Me reap the consequence of *their* thought. You cannot rescue others but only send them Love and your Will that one day they will see. Grieve not nor blame the consequence they bring to themselves for when their thought will change, the Truth will likewise reveal itself to them and all be healed, and fear no more shall wrestle these children of Me called 'men'.

Love and Will rightly come together in the heart. True acceptance always takes place in the heart; the head is too high to recognise the feelings of the Will and the lower centres are too wrapped up in their own anguish to openly accept the Light of heaven. Hence all that needs healing must come together in the Love and safety and acceptance of your heart. In the effort to heal, you deny the original cause of that which now needs to be healed. Always the cause is a reaction, a feeling, if you will. You cannot deny the feeling from existence for its energy remains but upon acceptance of its being you can transform the original energy to something now more suited to your Will.

Be joyous in your expression and that which it forms will bring joy. Your role here is not to deny form but to infuse it with the quality of spiritual intent. In all that you do, let this be the hallmark of you, that constant awareness of the higher being of you directs and infuses with the marriage of Love and Will all that you do. Beauty, honesty and Truth must as consequence flow through you, healing all that has been in pain, in your body and 'out' on what we have called the Earth plane.

The state of any manifested 'thing' must be changed in consciousness before it is changed in manifestation. This Truth contains all the knowledge you need to re-govern the affairs of your world, to heal that which man has tried to destroy of Earth and to bring righteous happiness and harmony into the processes of your day.

It is not enough that the small will of the human being state its desire. To change the state of something is far more than this. To truly know that something is, is to bring it about. But to work aright in the Earth plane, one must place one's focus and attention in that which is of a higher order than the normal human plane. Otherwise, how can your motive be devoid of the persuasions of the personality? The personality should be your tool, not your master. Ideologies are personality not soul driven. They exclude that which seems opposed and division is their basis, no matter how noble may sound their creed. The goodwill of the soul does not exclude. It recognises that each stands beside the other, that without all walls of a house, proper shelter cannot be provided for all. Such goodwill does not require effort on your part. It needs only a shift in consciousness to the plane of the soul and all effort is based on goodwill for such is the inclusive nature of the soul.

Interfere not with your brother's intent but include him in your intent. The effect is the same without the harm of coercion. To know him at the level of the soul is to know the right application of your intent and together, from the higher level of cause, you will influence the plane of effects. The personality has power over its own small intents but these are easily mastered by the intent of the soul, as is a drop of water swallowed and taken over by the ocean.

Love is a quality of soul. It drives out desire in an infusing Light of higher intent. With the 'twin' of its nature Will, it strengthens what is good in the small and weak, and burns away the unreality of negative and evil intent.

The Earth, as you must do, must change and grow, to re-form as new. Just as you can ease the passage of another, you can ease the changes of the Earth. Even more so, for the Earth is ever receptive to your Love where mankind is not always so! It is at the level of Love that man has dominion over the Earth, for in the end Love has dominion over everything and in identifying with Light or Love, does even one human being have power over matter. But remember that Earth is not just matter but a being itself, and behind all that constitutes the Earth is sentience. In this round of the Earth's being, it is Love which will transform the Earth and the clearing away of all that is negative from the Earth, in the sending of that negativity to Light, be it a seemingly ancient creature or curse, or a negativity imposed by man.

When a human stands on the rock of his soul and reaches far above to the divinity from which extends that soul, he can bring down healing the like of which has seldom been seen. For would but mankind know it, he is here on Earth to heal, not to selfishly exploit that which he finds on his doorstep, but to transform what he finds until it resonates to the sound of the highest Love his soul can intend.

So fear not the movement of mountains nor the rising or parting of the seas. Those things need your Love as much as you need Love to transform your personality to Light and change your life and others from sorrow to joy. Earth need never suffer from the wants of Man. When man changes the quality of his intent a whole new wisdom will reveal itself, and both Earth and humankind be blessed.

The Key

A keyhole is a way in or a way out. In this analogy, the keyhole is a place in the mind. The keyhole seems a tiny space for in your minds all is compartmentalised and to make the transition to another world, the pathway seems narrow and untravelled. Spirit is always the keyhole to another world. What other part of you is truly free? Of all the aspects you see as you it is the one that moves and crosses boundaries as it will.

Often these worlds seem to be pure colour or pure sound. As practice advances however, you see the colour of the sound, sound and light become one and the colour-sound a world is, *is* what it is. It requires no explanation of itself and none can be given. In your essence, at the purest part of you, you are this too, pure light and coloured sound, requiring not explanation nor justification.

Subtle, ah yes, the world of the spirit is subtle indeed and refined indeed is the practised eye that enters here. There is no key to this hole for the way is always open. It only seems closed because the clouds you place about yourself obscure it so.

A different shaped key will unlock a different door. The keyhole you create for your awareness will differ according to the quality of your consciousness. 'What you see is what you get' is a truism indeed. 'Sight' is perception. What you are able to 'see' depends on your level of consciousness. This is true even in the grossly physical world. Human emotion generates fogs so thick they are as effective in blocking your spiritual sight as physical fogs are in blocking your view of the world around you. Can you see then how the individual, and the mass of humanity, perpetuates its own blindness?

The key is the discovery of a door in your own consciousness that will take you beyond the cloudy confines of your emotional world. None who are driven by desires of the personality are free of these blinding mists, but the soul exists beyond these clouds of the astral world. The instant the soul and not the personality is the source of the directive, in that instant is clear sight found and the personality, its control given up to the soul, walks free, even in the planes of the physical world.

Is your key the shape of perfection? If not, how then can it give you a keyhole through which to experience perfection? Think of the key as the shape of your thought, your desire, your ambition. Whatever shape the key you create, there will be a keyhole it fits, for the creation of the key simultaneously creates the keyhole. This is the power of free will. Whatever mix of qualities shapes the key so will the experience be that you have unlocked for yourself.

Your 'desire' may be noble, it may have been inspired by your soul, but if you then mix it with qualities of fear, grandiosity and jealousy, these things too will shape your key and the experiential world you seem to step into be not the clear glorified world of the soul but the clouded fog that sits atop the human sea and you find yourself groping through these fogs once more or drowning in the emotions that brought them into 'being'. Leave these emotions outside the door, leave the personality behind when knocking at the spiritual door. With these things of the personal world clinging in bulk around you, how do you expect to enter in?

'Seek ye therefore the Oneness of me' is an invitation, not to abandon the Earth plane, but exist in it yet beyond its illusions. Its illusion is that *form* is the causal reality. Of course forms impact upon each other, just as the billiard ball collides with many others when hit by the cue. But it is consciousness that moves the cue. It is intent, of greater or lesser degree and wider or finer focus that brings action to the cue and the balls are affected to the measure and accuracy of that intent.

Your life is a plethora of billiard balls and your intent and focus the wielder of your cue. A tyrant has the focus of obsession, that is why his intent wrecks havoc where it will, for the weak (who are the many) have not will nor focus to match it, and man finds it hard to muster all his consciousness behind the good Will of a higher intent.

What to you are legitimate emotions—anger, praise, blame, love, discontent—are all masks of the fragile ego that sully the soul's intent. The intent of a higher plane must, to the unpractised, seem subtle indeed. To those newly practising this art of living under their soul's intent, it is seldom, at first, that the intent is not clouded, obscured by the ego's conflicting emotions and desires.

The ego's emotions are all based on fear. Even what it sees as love is underneath a fear for its love is predicated on a desire for the thing loved, in such a way that actions conveying that love are based on fear of losing it and strategies, games and manipulations are developed to 'protect' that love from loss. It is then subjected to jealousy, (another form of fear) possessiveness and control. Anything you name as 'love' which must be wreathed about with the grey matter of ego fear is not love at all. Seek ye therefore not 'love' as the ego of the personality knows it but Love of the unifying soul that discerns but does not discriminate in the way of the personality, its judgement being not what and when or how to withhold love but judgement of what is true and what is false.

Worry is also based on fear. It might be 'natural' to the ego/personality but it is unknown to the soul. What door does the key of worry unlock? What quality of energy does it bring to person or situation who is the object of your worry?

See you not that worry will help bring about the situation feared? Always return to the quality of your intent. If you would turn a situation of fear it must be seen as an image and replaced with images (imagination) of good Will and higher intent. Miracles are performed by those who see no fear but perceive only the higher intent, who give their Earthly perception up for the clear and holy sight of the soul. All that you perceive has its existence at some level or other of thought and if energy is to change anything it must come from changed thought.

Such a struggle it must seem to you when confronted every day by the heavy clouds of man's 'negative' emotional thought and the sheer size and 'weight' of such obscurity seems insurmountable by one so tiny and 'insignificant' as you. Yet your world abounds with examples of individuals who, advanced upon the path of the soul take their intent from the plane of the soul and achieve apparent wonders and miracles in the world of man, in healing and politics, the arts or any field in which they choose to make their stand.

Your intent in any endeavour is the key. It shapes the world the key unlocks for you. Does not the architect's intent determine the shape, function and beauty of a building? What would your cities, your countrysides and your lives be like if the intent of your citizens was souly led? Each time you see the clouds of man's emotional desire and personality deception for what it is—an illusion not of truth but of invention—you help to dispel these grey and sticky murks from Earth and clear a way with the sunshine of your soul intent.

Intent arises from Will. It is the main attribute or quality of Will with which you need concern yourself at this important time. Like anything to do with the unity of One, if you truly grasp the nature and mastery of this quality, you automatically acquire the rest, they being not separate.

In Will, intent is married irrevocably to discipline, persistence and what you see as 'courage'. Courage, in human terms is a little like hope in that it implies a possibility of lack, of 'not-courage'. In the domain of the soul, Will has no need of courage in the human sense for it has no fear of lack and therefore the sense of fear of failure that so plagues the human spheres has no place here.

Failure is an entirely human concept. There is no 'failure' on the higher planes. Failure is the inability to stay with the clarity of intent. It happens so easily in the way of the personality which switches constantly from one desire or 'intent' to another, creating a chaos of effects. The key to any door is your intent. The quality of your intent, as we have said, shapes the key, determines the door and chooses the world and consequence the key unlocks for you. If you would change the effects coming back to you then alter the quality of your intent and keep your attention, unwavering, upon the new intent. Your habits are what you have settled for. Too often they are the lowest common denominator of your intents. To change a habit is to become absorbed in a different intent.

To 'travel' to another realm enlarges your understanding and eventually enables you to be more effective on your physical plane. Is it not helpful when traversing unknown territory to be able to climb a hill and see the land ahead? Your sojourn in another realm provides you views of how the subtle patterns of the world are formed. The energies that form your life are then no longer a mystery but weaving patterns of colour and sound, and the landscape of Life within and without you becomes, not a haphazard mystery, but a subtle yet comprehensible display of thought in action. At all levels of being these patterns of colour and sound are moving. As you journey in other planes you learn the ingredients that end in your world as form.

Each journey you make through the keyhole to another realm purifies the 'you' that comes back to serve again, for did you not have to leave the bulky error of your thought behind to slip as Light through the keyhole of the door? When you return, do not re-clothe yourself in weight but use the Light of your new knowledge to dissipate the weight of previous 'knowledge' and so destroy that weight that sat before upon the world. Let it now be said that you are more than just your soul for even the soul has higher planes to go to, and glorious as it may be, it seeks glories greater far than these.

Great indeed are the cycles that turn upon your world, lifting in coloured spirals upon the wings of need. Humankind must find its way, along with many others for the kingdoms all move as one, leaving behind whence they have come.

By happy chance you may pass one day a keyhole to My kingdom and through its gap the Light and spacious clarity attract you in. Naked you go, stripped of all but the flame of you. Liquid it slips, a slither of light through the keyhole. The keyhole, a tiny gap through the walls of a plane that takes you through to another domain. Leave your tiny self behind if you would enter here for these planes know nothing of the dross with which you cloud your minds. In order to slip through this keyhole, leave all but your spirit behind. The keyhole to these higher planes is small indeed, the grossness of your world the camel to the needle's eye.

When you move through the keyholes of your higher mind, understanding deepens, subtlety holds sway, and the less and less it seems to have do with your 'everyday'. These higher realms are more still yet fuller their revelation, more difficult to 'lower' to the plane of Earth. Light indeed are the worlds beyond the key. Pure knowledge and the joy of knowing is the Light of these kingdoms in the planes of your mind where the grosser, selfish part of you cannot go.

These planes resound with the subtlest music and the essence of a colour which they are. These are the halls of learning, vaster far beyond the measure of your guess. Unbounded, their walls and ceilings each a universe express.

To be there is to know them, yet to truly know them you need forever. Forever has founded them, it is what they are. They are the rooms of thy Father's mansion.

Colour

Colours are the purest sound there is. To deal in colours
therefore is to deal with the real sound that something is.
True colour is not the manifested colour but the colour
behind the manifested colour. Because each *true* colour
is an expression of the One colour that *is*, a colour can be
called forth at need from the Oneness in which *all is*.

Each being is a unique combination of colour, the
shades and tones of its colour expressing the state of its
consciousness on any particular plane at any particular
moment. Since colour is an expression of a sound, what
has been said of sound is true also of colour. As awareness
moves from the strictly physical plane, colour and sound
can be experienced as one, and worlds of communication
open before the one aspiring to know.

To be healed therefore, is to change the colour and sound
emanating from one's inner core from those of disharmony
and discord to those that come directly from your immediate
source, your soul. To be one's true Self, one must emanate
one's true colour, not dwell in conscious disarray in a mixture
of colours gleaned from whatever emotional whirlpool
swirls across one's path or way. When caught in emotion,
ask what colour is your heart. When fired with zeal, ask
what colour is your heart. When filled with Love, what
colour is the soul? The colour of your love will alter
according to the quality that flows. Since God is Love

and He is all there really is, true Love must express all the colour there is, and Will express in manifested form all the power (sound) He is. All things that grow express the colour of the Love He is, if you would but see it.

Each system of the human body, each organ, each cell is colour. Each can therefore be influenced by the Mother colour it is. But its true colour emanates from the soul not from the mind or brain of the manifested body you see it as. To heal with colour then is to talk directly with the soul and let it choose for you the colour something really is, not in manifested form but that behind the form. Colour and sound, when properly understood contain all the true healing there is because they are what something truly is.

To cross the bridge into one's own soul is to find what no dis-ease or dis-harmony can resist. The colours tell you this is so. To know the true colour that something is, is to know its nature. To meet and immerse the mind in the colour that a thing is, is to understand it, for its colour, *being what it is*, must convey *directly* all that it is. Colour can be observed or absorbed. To admire and enjoy the colour of a flower as the eye sees it, is to gladden the heart and lift the spirit. To seek and immerse oneself in the true colour of the flower, is to gain knowledge of it, to understand it, to identify the intelligence of you with the beingness of it.

To know the colour that something is, one must, as with all true knowledge, be still. Then can its colour be invited to be absorbed into you and you into it. Only by dispassionate identification can something be truly known and understood behind the shifting forms and projections of the world. In such a way can you know the quality of a thing, and when something is met by a still mind it cannot influence that mind. In this point of stillness you change not, as God, which is Still-ness, changes not. So if you would truly know the world, but be free of it, you must be still, not in movement, but in chasing after desires and projections of the tiny mind. And soon, when

you have learned to see the colour of the world, you will hear
its sound as well, and you will know someone or something
by the sound it makes. You will hear its loveless crashing or
the sweet of Love's refrain, for truly the world is made of
sound, and all things sing of their colour's sound.

Every sound that springs forth from God has colour.
Each wave that is God's thought is colour. Behind every
level of cause and effect is a change of colour. A level or
plane is simply a stage of a wave's journey, a 'place' along its
course as it is flung out from God. As the wave concentrates,
the farther it is flung, the more changeable and 'solid' it
becomes. As waves concentrate, they form, in whatever
pattern dictated by their song which dictates the speed,
direction and twist of the wave. The wave, imprinting itself
on the substance of God, creates its own boundaries, the
complement of itself coming back to it and keeping it in
shape. As a consciousness yourself, you can perceive a wave
at any stage of its journey into concentration. This is what, in
fact, the higher and lower parts of yourself do. They perceive
being at different stages of the journey as God's waves.

Here, where you sit, in the densest concentration of the
waves, you feel bound, caught in this complex set of waves
of colour and sound. Your own thought amplifies the sound
you take in, in what your senses think is real, thinking
and acting accordingly, thus producing more concentrated
waves, waves of solidity, of materiality. 'Letting go' of
materiality is the non-production of such waves, so that
you do not add to the lower levels of being.

When your thought is trained to stay on higher mind,
only the larger, lighter waves emit from you, thus 'raising'
the world because they do not exist at or add to the lower
planes. At any level a wave will find itself in company of
similar waves. It must be this way when you remember that
experience is simply your perception, the resting of your
attention at a point along a wave. To train your attention

is to give yourself the Kingdom of God. Your attention to qualities of thought gives you your experiences of life, and keeps you bound in the slow, concentrated end of Life's waves or sets you freer, extant in the higher bands of His thought, through expansion and Light to the stillpoint wherein each thought *is*, and whereto each thought has or has not come. The illusion of manifested being disappears into knowledge in the unseen Light.

Each colour is a world of its own. Each is complete unto itself even though it is only one of the colours that God is. These colours, being also sound, are the energy or force that drives and determines the length, direction and shape of a wave. Everything in the manifested universe may be a combination of colours, so when you perceive them, they will appear changeable and complex, according to which of their component colours you are accessing at a particular moment. But go to the source of their component colours and you will know those things in their purity and unchangeable nature.

The world of pure colour is light and expanding. The colours you see in the physical world are but a reflection of their concentration. Whatever you 'see' in the physical world is a reflection. That is why the more still you are the more clear is the reflection shown to you or revealed in you. As these things are not fully comprehensible in words we must use analogies and likeness to help you to the point where they will be revealed to you in the fullness of understanding.

Colour is a key to My kingdom; not colour as you know it in the world but as your soul is composed of it, light, expanding and free.

What shapes a person's colour is his relationship with God. Personality has a different colour from soul, but when the personality is brought consciously under the direction of the soul, its colours change and whirl, still profligate at first maybe, but then they harmonise, and the bodies of the personality begin in unison to serve the purpose in truth appointed them. The colour you are shows that you are an aspect of the rainbow of Me. In all colours you will find Me, yay, even in black, for am I not all that there is and therefore naught can be that is truly opposition to Me. Yet it seems not, for dark and stormy indeed seem the colours of some, and evil indeed seems doomed to haunt the lives of men. Yet in Truth even evil must transmute to its true nature—Me—who is Light, in the end.

Colour and sound are the language of Me. They are before words that all may know directly the nature of all that proliferates and apparently 'descends' from the planes you call divinity to form and shape the plane of materiality. I tease not for teasing implies deceit and I do not deceive. I laugh though, for laughter sets you free. Laughter is the sound of many colours for it runs across the rainbow of My Love like scales, and you might as well have dipped yourself in Light for laughter takes you straight away to everybody's soul.

Healing

That which does not concern you is ever the worry of others. You can do nothing for their path, only for your own. If you are as a light and they seek to shine in that light, *their* way will be illumined and by their raising of themselves you too will be lifted. But if they choose to heed not the brightness before them to help their way let it trouble you not. Sympathy and pity do not elevate. Only Love does that, but only if the one who is loved avails himself of it. No Love that you give is lost. Being what God is, it is imperishable. It simply serves to clear the fogs of doubt built like a wall around the lives of men. It can therefore be used at any time to restore *reality* to one willing to receive it, willing to see the Truth of it instead of the foggy wall that blinds the eyes and stops the ears. Take heart then that naught is lost of your efforts. All that is true stays in Truth and the false will disappear when its lack of power is acknowledged.

Do you not see how your Love does not act nor move? It *is* and therefore is always available regardless of time or space, to which it has no application. Love as God loves cannot be temporal, therefore is not subject to the laws of temporality. This is the basis of a miracle. A miracle is Love which being what God is, transcends time. It is always there, available as *reality* for those open to accepting it. It changes nothing in time because it is outside of time yet is available to any who think they exist only in time, because in truth they share its reality. How can they not, since God is Truth, God is Reality and there *is* nothing outside of the Truth that He is. Sorrow and loss are human emotions. They are not known in the higher spiritual planes. The God-realised man does not experience the sorrows of the world. How can he when he is realising only God which knows no lack? Compassion does not recognise lack as a reality, but as an error. Thus it allows for Love to take the place of judgement and censure.

When one who commits crimes against his brothers realises Love, he knows his error and his regret may be great. In this sense, punishment of itself is useless and is merely an attempt at vengeance by the ignorant. What prisoner of hate could long withstand the concerted Will of Love from his fellow-man? If one by one your wrong-doers were subjected to the *unrelenting* Love of his peers, not admonition, pity or fear, which are all human distortions of the only emotion that God is, (Love) he would not long be able to stand against its power for being what God is it is omnipotent. The pure, non-judgmental Love of God heals because it is wholeness and wholeness must encompass all its parts.

So little you know of Truth and Love! A person may know the Love of wholeness but still leave the Earth. Such a 'death' is choice, not of capitulation to lack, but a recognition of time and lessons learned and passed by way of the physical life. Love is Life. Therefore, when Love is withdrawn from the physical effects of life, these effects must wither. No matter how great a love you have for another, if they do not have Love for themselves or accept it via others, your Love will not serve to keep them wholly on this plane. Sickness is the withdrawal of the consciousness of Love to one or several of its body's parts, a withdrawal of Love from an aspect of Life.

Whatever part or system of the body expresses that aspect of Life will be then affected by its lack. The 'mechanical' fixing of the body through pills, potions and medical 'practice' is simply a substitute for the withdrawn Life-force that the body system now lacks.

The Love of which we speak is seldom realised by man. Such is its power that it obliterates all other human consciousness from the mind it occupies. For most it can seldom be sustained for more than an instant or two, yet its practise will bring untold value and would quickly transform any who dared to hold it more than an instant in their hands. This is not the small love of human desire of which we speak, but Life itself. It never demands but only serves, because it can only give out in increase, not take away nor suck in. Yet it will destroy, but that which is destroyed by Love was never part of Truth, and lies are ever blown away by right, as shadows cannot abide where nothing blocks the Light.

Healing, it is said, is 'making whole'. But in Truth, in the Reality that is forever, wholeness already *is* and what is real is already whole. You do not need to make it so. It is *you* who are in Reality whole and your wellness depends only on your recognising this as so. So simple is this Truth that the mind of man cannot accept it. The intellect, wishing for 'autonomy' from what it sees outside itself—namely 'God'—looks always for complicated constructs of its own, complicated answers to justify its inventions. Thus it has involved you in a complex web of deception from which it seems only enormous effort can extricate you.

The effects of Life are so various you have thought Life itself to be complex, but it is in fact the simplest thing. If you would have the wondrous effects of Life at your fingertips then it is the simplicity of Life you must seek. Life and Love can be said to be the same thing. Love is simply the 'driving force' of Life, which is why it must *heal* when used and understood. So practise Love, which obliterates all else; fear, doubt and illness. It is not a 'love' which crushes out the will of others. It is harmless, yet its power is total. It does not presuppose an outcome as outcomes arise from it as a natural consequence, and you cannot try to order the outcome of Love without stepping outside of Love and into desire, thereby becoming human, not divine.

Love cannot judge because judgement is divisive; it chooses between actions whereas Love simply *is*. Because it is and does not act, the actions or outcomes that appear to flow from it must be expressions of its wholeness and since wholeness is of God it is necessarily unknowable in its entirety, by man. You cannot therefore, order or predict the right outcome of Love, but it is true faith to know that Truth, Love and God are all the same thing and therefore the answers to all the large and petty problems of man.

Fear is of this world, it blocks the higher view and works subtly in your veins to destroy even the perfection of the body over which you should by right have command of all aspects. Take heart for 'heart' indeed is the key to all physical demands at this time in your world.

Love is its own protection. A body so loved that not one part of it is neglected is amour impenetrable to the 'forces' that, given a pathway, will disease and destroy. We speak not of vanity disguised as love but a pure Love for the instrument of creating as an aspect of God in this world. Yet you teach your children not love of their bodies but fear. Do you heap upon your friend blame, weakness and fear, and then expect him to return joy, devotion and strength to you? Yet in your physical world, who is your closest friend but your body? Does the painter not have to care for his brushes and the musician his instrument or they will not produce the painterly or musical effects their players seek to create in the world?

You cannot command that which does not respond to you. Do not stay so high above your body that it is treated as an appendage of you and not, as is the truth, part of the chain of the causal command arising from your soul. Where Love is, fear—with its many faces and guises—cannot be. Love your body therefore, not with potions and lotions, but with Love emanating from inside, and in this Love you will find gratitude for its service. Judgement and expectation will fall away, and thus the antidote to all your physical ills be found.

Such Love is not a light matter but a matter of Light. It links you directly and unswervingly to the source or soul of you, and empowers you in the physical world, providing a right channel for the proper function of *you*. Love and gratitude for the body must never be withheld through perception of apparent fault. A part not seen as whole by you has no fault, it is an end result, not the cause of its own malaise. You do not berate your car for not going when it has no fuel! Love is your fuel and gratitude its elder child. If you cannot find Love for what you think is not whole, then give gratitude for the lesson. Love must follow, and as you pour it out from within upon the physicality of you, you cease to be affected by an echo and take charge instead of the causal consciousness that is you. Then Love and Will can marry, and the active Intelligence of God applies itself in every part of your body, and spirit is infused in matter through the instrument of *you*.

If you approach the body with ideas of lack, how can the door of true healing be unlocked for you? If you are in command of your consciousness how can it return other to you than that which you indulged in? Your body as well as all other levels of the manifestation of your being, is a complex pattern of waveforms. That pattern is determined by the *quality* of the energy that sends it forth. Consciousness is always the source of energy. The purity and health of the soul can, when the channels are mastered, create whatever ideal in the body you seek.

Do you not see how you can never cease to be? You may come through fire and death and still 'be'. Your body may be mutilated, your mind disordered, and all that you held dear may have disappeared, yet you still 'be'. Your being depends not on these outer things and will still be when they pass away. It shakes not as a mountain does, to slide in the wake of time into the sea.

Triumphant are they who stay not in the circumstance but see their pain only as experience, and know that each step, though gruelling it may seem, adds feathers to their wings. One day when they have realised they do indeed have wings, their mountain top of worldly strife is reached and never more upon the ground of suffering they tread but spread their wings and fly upon the spirit's air, alighting only when they wish to spread their wings of Love as a shelter there for climbers on the ground still struggling up their mountain, homeward bound.

Fear is the resistance of Love. It is the most damaging of all inventions of man. It is the most deeply held belief of man's attempt to separate himself from other aspects of Life, from the beings that are Life, and from the Truth of what he himself is. Yet fear is more quickly dissolved by Love than ice is melted by a flame. Resistance to Love—that is, Truth—is, in whatever form it takes, the sole cause of ill, from the tiniest anxieties to the greatest phobias. Irritation, anger and blame, all are resistances to the outflowing of divine Love which is Life. How deeply you have buried your hearts in the dark! Your solidity of fear tightens muscles, tenses organs, spills a flow of chemical poison through the body's tiny pathways. How can your body live in health if Life cannot flow through it? It is after all, only a conduit constructed as are your plumbing pipes to convey water or your wires electricity. You bathe the outside but when do you cleanse within?

To bathe the body-mind with Love is more beneficial by far than any attempt to tinker in its workings through the inventions of man, but you teach your children not this Life-giving thing, wasting time instead on habits that increase their fears. Teach them to shelter themselves with Love, that nothing can register negatively flowing in when Love is flowing out. The mind cannot pay attention to Love and fear at the same time. Each instant, you make a choice on which path you live. Love is not submissive, it is power.

But it *is* submission to give up fear, and letting in the flow of Love, submit to Life itself. This is what it means to serve. Real service must be to the greater Will.

So hard you make them, the choices of the world. So little chance you give yourselves to really play, for Love is play, a wondrous tumbling out of endless Life. When you know such lightness will you join the ranks of those who live in higher planes, and through these tumbling, spilling, energetic games will humanity transform and innocence evolve to mantle Earth with Love.

The Path

The rituals which are ever the concern of men are not the concern of God and should not allow the genuine seeker to be distracted from his destination and his own chosen way. Use and choose as you will. It matters little in the long run if your path be straight or diverging. Only your sense of time is affected and time is nought in the abode of the Lord.

A master is here to guide you. He does not own your path, nor does he lay down rules for your obedience, but appears always as a loving support as and when it is required for your peace of mind and encouragement of progress. Loyalty to a master therefore is required only in so far as you wish to give it. The soul is always free to join, to come and go as it will. Only the certainty of the destination is not in dispute. Wisdom gathered along the way merely short circuits the route.

While there are a multitude of paths to the Truth, reason will show there is only one right path for you. You are, after all, a unique wave of Light and how can you move except within your own wave? You are the tourist on the end of your elastic cord of Light and must bounce back whence you came. In consciousness only, not in Reality, are there separate parts of you. All the masters in the many worlds cannot walk your path for you, and while you may admire and wish to emulate their strengths, it is to your own higher Self you must return. It waits for you, separate not in some far off and distant land but, 'beside and all around,' closer if you would but see it, than all your fears. A step a little to the side of dread it waits, ever mindful of God for it is Light, or God, where it dwells, and Light whereof the substance it is made.

Seek not then the teachings of another except to remind yourself that the journey possible can be made, in fact no journey, but a return to mindfulness that you are what you have always been, and your soul resides, an intermediary between the Light and what, in Earthly terms, you know as you.

Be pressured not then into the servitude of another's way for each is a band of Light, all of which together constitutes mankind, and all are joined not at the outer perimeter as one, but at their source of Light. Only the infusion of their consciousness with that Light shall make them one. The rightful work of a group therefore is on the higher planes. On Earth this work is effective only in so far as each can stay within the Light of his own higher Self and soul. Then the will of the personality serves the higher good and no question of fanaticism, or following of leadership which is 'evil,' guessed as just but distorted in intent, can sway you from the path of your own soul and higher Self which wait unchanged for your recognition.

It makes no difference to the Truth whether you recognise it, but your recognition of the Truth will give you experience of joy, where failure to see it can only bring you pain. It is the nature of this physical plane to settle into patterns for it is patterns that maketh the plane. The personality, functioning as it is in this plane, settles quickly to its patterns, but if it is to be brought under the Will of the soul, it must be frequently 'knocked off' its own course to be forced to follow or construct a more useful pattern that for the moment better serves the soul's higher purpose and Being's greater good. Yet much distress and fear is built around these changes in your pattern. What you see as knocks in life may be in fact a prod to change your view.

In this only is the disciple tested, but never by God. What use has God for scoring you? Project not onto God that small ignoble thinking that belongs to those far-flung parts of you. God is undivided and makes not divisions of rank or race between you, does not exclude parts of Himself from 'heaven' which is after all Himself too! Nay, laugh, but have compassion for the fears of others who cannot see the all inclusive goodness of God, the undivided total of Being, which remains true of all worlds and planes beyond appearance and perception of the form.

Go then with glad heart and when a push for change wobbles hard your point of view, adapt. Find those boulders in your way, constructed not to foil or tarry you, but see 'tis your soul itself that molds your path; a nudge from above, around and inside of you to see the way anew. The boulders in your stream are patterns. Once, when new, they were stepping stones to pathways higher, and now are blocks to help you find a pattern new. They are not in this sense even the construction of the soul but a natural outcome of the way—the gradual mastery of soul over that which functions here as 'you'. Like the fish that swims upstream you can swim around them, leap over them or hide a while behind them, hoping for some shelter from the stream. In Truth, you are not fish, but stream.

It is your relationship with your Will that creates your path. When you misunderstand, repress or thwart your Will, your path becomes 'rocky' as 'boulders' form in your way. Boulders are circumstances or events designed to demonstrate to you how you have mishandled Will. They are created by you in that they are the consequences of your thought-action returning to you. They are not, however, an excuse for lamentation or self-criticism. Such a response only serves to create new boulders in your way. Nor are they an excuse to blame others, or God, for your mischances in the world. That similarly will obscure the lighted way. Instead, examine the lesson in Light of your Will. What aspect of your Will does this boulder thwart, for that aspect is truly that part of you, you have denied. Remember that although right use of *your* Will is never harmful to others, it never means subjugation, (which is denial) of your Will, either.

What darkness can exist when Light is shone upon it? It may cower in its exposure but it is still no longer dark as it was. Shine Light upon all the mischief of the world and it shall disappear. Bring your Will into the Light of your Love and you will see all things differently.

How can the abundance of God be yours if you align not to the Will which brings that abundance into manifestation for you? This is why we say that to have a quality you must be that quality. You cannot have something you are not prepared to be, for that is the nature of being. The key and the world it unlocks are One. This must be since God is undivided. Have we not said that to drink of the cup of hatefulness a world of hate hits back at you? And so it is with all qualities; friendship is the key to a world of friends, appreciation the key to a universe of appreciation. Appreciation is a form aspect of Love and must echo back and forth to you that which is appreciated.

The qualities of all that you aspire to be are God's qualities. They are what God is. How could they not be? If it is sight that you wish to heal in yourself know that God *is* sight. God is the ability to see. When you identify *your* sight with the quality called sight that is God's, your sight will be healed. You will know that which is a quality of the divine cannot be faulty, and in your identification with it, neither can *your* sight be faulty. When you know yourself as One with God, you have the attributes of God, and all that is designed to function in the world as you, must function perfectly. If you want to heal your eyes, identify not with them, but with the quality of sight which God is. To identify with something is to know yourself as that. Such is the power of human consciousness that as you climb the ladder of awareness you become transformed and that which radiates from you likewise touches and transforms.

When you truly identify with that which is perfect you cannot be anything but perfect in your manifestation. In Truth there is no separation, and the attributes of the One must be the attributes of the many. Only in your consciousness do you fall from grace and know yourself as less that what you truly are. The framework of human thinking is built on a logic of impossibility, and until the basis of your thinking changes, naught but sorrow shall beset your world and the hand of death appear to rob the joy from you.

Whatever you identify with, you are, for that is the nature of being and the gift of free will. God *is* the universe. What He is, is yours. Identify with God and what seems to be below God, like your body, flows and functions as it should. Your body is the 'end' of your wave. God is its cause. Know your Self as the cause and your body cannot but obey.

You seek that which is familiar, thus valleys of darkness and despair entrap you. You visit there through habit. To strike new pathways to the Light takes courage, not for any danger lying in the journey but to turn aside repeatedly from habit, to train the personality to find another way whilst all about you others flounder who remain in well worn ways.

Raise your mind, raise it to where all is Light and what does now seem dark will be illuminated without effort. 'Doing' is in truth a radiatory effect of 'being'. The quality and effectiveness of your doing therefore is a direct result of your state of being. It is this radiatory effect of being which gives intent its causal function. Your state of being in any instant is your intent. Your lives, indeed your world, are the effect of your being—your intent. The spiritual disciple is so called because of the discipline for which a change of habit calls.

True will is not rampant emotion, which in fact is thwarting of Will. Appreciate your Will, give it thanks for being and you will discover your wholeness on this plane, and it will become as heaven to you. Nothing is difficult when you accept and appreciate your Will.

Appreciation of Will is the key to being on your Earth plane at present, for this appreciation marries the pillars of being and stands you independent of the vagaries of other men. It stands you upon the rock of undivided soul and opens the door to freedom, linking the paths of Earth and heaven, and you move, not in scared and doubtful shadows but surety of Light, seeking not the next excitement, nor the path through tangled doubt, for the way is already clear, stretching not ahead but all around. You stand on it already, needing no movement for your being is found.

Service

How can you spiritually 'progress' unless you leave the personal behind? In Truth you have no personality. In Truth you are not your personality any more than you are your body. Your body, emotions and personality have simply been tools to get you functioning on this plane. They are, as in transport, a bicycle must precede an aeroplane. Just as it is inappropriate to cycle across the world instead of catching a plane, if you have need of haste, so it is inappropriate when desiring to transmute your life to functioning on higher levels, to use the lesser pathways travelled by these form-bound aspects of you.

When you give up these separated aspects of yourself and give control to the higher intent of you, you cannot help but function, (yes even on the Earth plane) for that which is of greater good for all that live in the world with you. What is seen as service in your plane (the plane of the personality) is to the higher levels the Truth, and therefore the true art of being.

Sacrifice does not exist in the eyes of God, for Love ever lays itself at the feet of another, yet loses nothing of itself in so doing. Sacrifice is the idea of loss, that something must be given up in the act thereof. But Love is self-perpetuating. It diminishes not for being given away, for how can what is the nature of divine Creation diminish by being what it is?

Yet service in Love is never weak for right spiritual practise retains discernment. Discernment springs naturally from knowing the difference between the eagerness of the personality and Love that is divine. The latter is available and knows when to step forward, whereas the former rushes in, judging, not always appropriately, what is right at any given time.

Service is a threefold thing. The personality must serve the soul and the soul must serve in turn the divinity of thee. Beyond these three are other trinities for the vastness of God's being knows no limit, and service thus, as an attribute of Love, is boundless. Likewise, miracles have no end, for miracles and service are the rippling action of Love. Love itself moves not, being the nature of God which moves not but *is*. That is why divine Love is always available to you, to all the creatures in the universe beside you, to every space that fills the night and every light that lightens day, for as an attribute of God how can it not be intrinsic in all that is, in Truth, expression of God?

Service may appear to be an action but actually it is a state of mind. It stands neutrally in Love, and being a state, as Love is, it is always ready. Because it is a quality, often it requires only that the one needing service should dip himself briefly in its calm waters to find a change of mind, and thus the service is performed.

So closely aligned are service and Love, are they in fact distinguishable at all? True service never martyrs itself nor performs unwillingly for others, for then it is not service but duty, an act of conscience, not a lifting of consciousness. How can this be, that true service is Love? Because Love—being an attribute of God—contains *all*, it nurtures totally, and therefore answers all need. And what is service but the answering of need? Of course service may appear as action, but it is action which remains rooted in the stillness of Love. It is however, never remote, nor dismissive, but warm enough to heat the chilliest day and light enough to brighten the darkest cave. You need not seek to serve, it grows naturally from a state of Love. Love, grace and service are simply different windows on the same thing.

What is true for one must be true for all when Truth is recognised as Truth and form as form, but the feeling life of man excludes, cuts some out and lets some in. The Love and joy of soul excludes not any life nor any man. You ignore these priceless pearls and hanker after 'more', seeing not that comprehension of one Truth must lead you to the rest since Truth is One and whole, not divided, not separated as you in your separated consciousness expect.

The emotions of man are his barriers to seeing God in other men. The small joys and pleasures—'love' and hate and want for gain—mask the Truth of higher planes. They complicate the simple and pass for freedom what is bound in chains. Service to humanity does not wallow in the emotions, no matter how personally rewarding they may at times appear to be. The true reward of service is an experience of all three attributes of the divine as it manifests in this round of your world today; Divine Love, Will and the right activity of Intelligence of higher mind. When you understand clearly the nature of these three, you overcome the difficult, build bridges across the mires of conflict, drown not in the ego's emotional sea, and truly build structures of energy that raise the thought and circumstance of humankind. Only through the proper balance of all these can the real work on Earth be done.

Ever the hard way do you wander when you do not let us steer your heart. The heart steered from above has no need of hope, it has the surety of Love. The focus you need on the lower planes is a view of the higher Self of you for is not the better guide the one who sees the greater view? The great Ones wield their power in colour and sound with purity of intent. What colours and sounds are the thoughts which drive your life? Is your life driven by others? Service is not acquiescence, it is the throwing of your power behind the greater good. It is the offering of your energy of colour and sound, (the children of the quality of your intent) to the greater service, like the energies of those masters who serve the greater purpose of your world.

Joyful is the welcome received by the humble hearted! When you come to us in humbleness, you leave behind false pride, the pride which puts barriers between you, which has to elevate you above the rest, but falsely. To truly help another, one must be humble, recognising in another your own folly and weakness of resolve. When the Light is truly shining in your eyes you cannot see evil, just the stumbling of one who has lost their way.

Humility is strength because it recognises greatness that is greater than itself alone, yet neither is it weak, for knowing itself a part and product of that greatness it is great indeed. Its strength is true for it is built on identification with unity, standing as it must in the One that divides not. Take a moment and bask in the joy of your welcome here in the planes of the soul where humility opens the door to uniqueness fully known, and you stand amongst the truly equal, for how amongst the One Son of God can this equality not be?

Humility is not a sacrifice of things held dear but an understanding of what is truly so. Humility lies in unity. It is not an offering to be attacked. It is not martyrdom which seeks praise for its self-righteousness. Rarely today is a true martyr to be found, free of clinging righteousness and glamorous intent. The humble are grateful to have found a key to home. Home, they find, is not a long struggle away, but with them all the time. Where else could a greater welcome be but in the arms of those who have waited patiently to have those of their number once missing, home.

Humility is strength because it submits to that which is stronger than itself. Tyranny is not strength because it does not recognise wholeness, does not see the other as part of itself. It does not therefore have the power of Oneness which in Truth is all there is. If it is not part of Truth then it must be temporal and illusory. Humility must serve because it recognises itself as part of the whole and wholeness cannot be without each part supporting the others. How can you, as part of the One, not be supported by the rest? Being Truth, this is an automatic quality of the higher planes which is why when you attain consciousness of those planes they uplift you so, and give you feelings of support and integration with the lightness of Truth. And this is why none of the subjects of this book can *really* be separate from the others except for intellectual purposes.

It is your feelings of separateness that are an illusion on your plane. In Truth even here you are not separate from those others in the world with you. You have paid so much attention to the effects, the echoes you sense around you, that you overlook the Truth that they have the same cause, Life itself. Diversity is an expression of aspects of the whole. How can infinite possibility—God—not be expressed as infinite diversity? Humility recognises the unbreakable bonds that hold you to the rest of what *is*. That is why it contains no arrogance yet avails itself of all the power of Oneness. But the submission of humility is not to any sort of tyranny, great or small, which is an effect of 'separation,' because humility does not recognise tyranny as real.

Fear then, need have no place in your hearts. What is there to fear? Death does not exist, your beingness goes on forever, and your glory grows with every rise upon the ladder of consciousness. The key to healing—Love—is also yours, for Love must be the nature of wholeness, therefore Love must make whole, heal.

Go now and find the being of thee. Stop, when the world says 'go,' and rest in the peace of Me. Fear nothing, but stand on the rock where your soul rests in Me.

Being

Being is a state not an action. Since you *are* God expressed as the individual you, whatever it is of God you express, so the nature of your being must be. As God moves not, but only *is*, so it must be with the beingness that you are. Those things about you by which you identify yourself—a body, personality, behaviour and activities of mind—are not the unchangingness of you, rather, they are the echoes of your experimentation with possibilities. God moves not but only appears to do so. So it is with you. Your being sits firmly in God, for it is God. What else can it be since nothing but God *is* in Reality. Your being is in that Still, uncreated potential that God is.

You cannot *seek* to know your being for seeking is an action and an action is not what being is. Knowledge of your being will not come to you through victory in war, success in business or through ascetic practise. It is already there, not for discovery but for uncovering. Your actions are like shadows on a wall, they will not show you the depth and dimension, the colour or subtlety of that which casts them two-dimensional and black.

The most that being can 'do' is to have a quality of intent. This is its sifting through the potential that God is. This is the 'thinking' process of being, Being exploring itself. Yet even in this it has moved not. So far have you flung your attention from the beingness of you that you have caught yourself in a web of your own echoes. You rush in endless fascination from one reverberation of the web to another, thinking yourself to be the spider, when in fact you are the world in which the spider is contained.

The 'realised soul' is one who has turned away from the world of echoes to return his awareness to the singer of the song, mastered the restlessness of a habit of wandering, and come home instead to experience the endlessness of what he has, in Truth, always been.

You exist on all planes simultaneously. Freedom on all planes comes from acceptance of those aspects of yourself manifesting on each plane. You cannot master being on each plane unless you are conscious of being there. If you would not live as a man sitting in a box, you must see the box, as well as the meadow in which it sits. A box binds, limits and forms. It falsifies a barrier where none need exist. If you would alter the shape and properties of your box you must see that it is there. Should you decide to destroy it, to reconvert it to the 'air' from which you created it, again, you must first see that it is there.

You built the box from the echo of your own Will. Your vaster Will gives you not the box but the meadow and all the worlds beyond. Will you not journey with that greater Will? Will you not explore with Me the greater flights of higher mind where sound and colour build the universe, where all who travel high are blessed with wings of speed, their power no less great than that which held the sun in mind or flung the stars to light the black of rest? To think that being is confined to that which you can see is perhaps the biggest temptation of error available to entrap humankind. From this error so many errors of the personality arise.

God is all there is in Truth and therefore God is also all the possibility there is. God then is All potential, and in Truth already contains that potential. Herein lie the secrets of mastery, of governance of soul over tiny self, of triumph of faith over hope, and the mechanism by which all that is known as evil can be shut away from the experience of the world.

That which is your highest desire already is. All the qualities of God already are. They wait not on your enlightenment to be called into existence. They wait not on your hope that at some future moment they will appear in miraculous rescue, and they depend not on your recognition for their existence. Their effect in your lives however, depends on your knowledge that they *are*, and their manifestation in your life is a measure of the constancy with which you *know* they already are.

This is the gift of Godhood. As an expression of God, you are all that God is, and have all that God is. Right asking therefore is not a prayer of pleading but a constant knowing that your desire is met, for in the potential that God is it already exists, and waits not upon *your* circumstance or recognition to be. This is why the right focus of your attention is so important, because whatever you know to be, *is*, and sooner or later, in measure of your faith, (your knowledge that it is) it will manifest. Thus even before you thought of it, the shape of the key was imprinted on the substance of God and therefore it was granted you before you asked. Successful prayer is not a pleading to God for change or recognition, but a knowledge constantly known, that in the potential of God the prayer was answered, even before its asking.

To know being as God knows it, is the challenge of the tiny mind of mankind. To live by the Laws of God is not to live under restriction of constraint defined by your fellow man, even when they try to sanctify their rules by the name of God. To live God-like is to understand that which God is, and to function aright is to know that God is all potential, all Love, and that the second, Love, contains the first, and from this understanding follows all right thought, action and manifestation. Being is what God is, not in the past or the future, but always *now*, and all that you desire, even when in dark despair, is already granted. How could it not be, when God is all there is?

Pass it onto others, this joy of being. Try to contain it or resist it and it will feel as if a battle starts within. But open your pores and let it seep out, and you will find it sparkling the very air around, going before you as a light around a candle, for it is in fact a candle, lit within. Let it seep out, gently rising from the depths of each centre, for at the core of each centre of you is beingness itself, and at its heart being is joyfulness.

Since being is endless, for that is what God is, so must its nature—joy—be endless, and the well of it inside you therefore be without measure, and only inattention bring about its apparent lack. The joy of being can be as bursting as a giant waterfall or gentle as a butterfly on air. Whatever its expression, it remains sure of itself, as unshakeable as the foundations of the world are not for they are but a temporal thing, and Being, as it is that we call 'God,' will be forever. Thus it was promised He would be with you even unto the end of the world.

First find your soul, and then seek the higher Self or Spirit of you. Always your challenge is to infuse that which is 'lower' with that which is higher and Lighter. How else will you light the dark recesses of yourselves and your world except with Light? Learn to trust the spirit of your being but be constantly aware of the glamours of personality intent. Such glamours divert the novice from true understanding. You can recognise a glamour by its separative intent. A glamour tries to elevate you unjustly, places barriers between you and others, and seeks attention for the gain of self, no matter how small, instead of the advancement of all.

Your being is rich with possibility. Be guided then by its centrality and lose yourself not in the delusions of form. Transmuted, nothing dies. Do not presume to know what your Spirit wants for you. Only from above can you see what you are. Let the Love and service of your higher Self guide your intent, and all the worlds of God's possibility open before you, ceasing time but commencing play.

The joy of being need never leave you. Above all sorrows and tribulations of the world it can remain. Beingness is immortality. It is before time was and is evermore when time ceases. For time does cease my friends, when you tarry not in its multitude of change. Only in physicality is change, and as degrees of physicality recede so does everlasting Being be.

Think not therefore on the worries of the day but plant your feet firmly in the muds of change and keep your heart and head in heaven, that what is high 'above' the world of change may filter down, infuse the mud of ages with the light of freedom gained, and turn to angel dust the muddied waters of God's farthest realm. So all of Earth shall sing, its pain forgot, its spirit fly in flowering glory, raised from Earth to heaven.

Epilogue

To Soul

Glorious is my own soul that liveth ever in God
Glorious is the being which I AM
For in me dwells the everlasting that I AM
The bridge across forever belongs to me
How can it not?
For it is who I AM
And only fear of greatness sunders it from me

Gratitude will build this bridge anew
And naught can break what I have forged with You
So gently still my heart when doubt does blind my view
And take my hand that gropes in vain for You
Lead my feet across the bridge
That I may know myself as part of You.

Book III

I AM within and without
I AM in all things
And therefore we are One

Introduction

Relationship is both the reality and the illusion of the separated world. Think deeply on this in light of what has elsewhere been said in these volumes and you will begin to understand the source of much of man's confusion.

Reality is that which is in operation on any one plane and so it patterns, conforms, binds and restricts the experience and perception of those who feel themselves existing on that plane. Reality, with a capital 'R' may also refer to Truth, or that which lies behind the outer form or experience of a plane. Stretching outward from the source, lie many planes of reality, and likewise, evolving back towards the source are many others. You can see then, as we have said, each plane has its own reality and its own illusion. Illusion is the inability to see beyond the plane one's consciousness occupies, to the fact of other planes. It is also the assumption that the interrelationships between those parts occupying a plane are of a particular nature.

In the evolving worlds all is change, and these worlds are webbed in varying degrees of Light as they raise their consciousness, transmuting their substance from density to lightness. At each level of being, at each density of substance, these worlds are internally moving, the relationship of one part to another alternately held in balance and moved to a new balance. Each has its own internal order and the paths of raising travelled by its parts are laid down by the laws which created it, those laws being both its nature and its limit of activity. Each solar system and each world within each solar system has a basis of existence fundamental to itself yet set within a greater law of physicality governing the various planes of consciousness through which it passes on its journey of consciousness.

Each world is a being containing many beings and these worlds in turn contained within a greater being. As it is in the microcosm, so it is in the macrocosm and this law holds, be it within your body or the body of the planet, the sun, or 'your' solar system as the body of a greater whole. Beyond any man's comprehension is the relationship between the great solar beings and the higher journeys of *their* souls, and yet eventually, contained as you are within the greater life of these majestic beings, you will one day *know*, but then you will be joined, not as separate men, but conscious units of this greater whole.

It is not your comprehension of these greater matters that is required at present, but your acceptance of the bigger plan, that you may in bright awareness play your part, and so in ordered speed advance your human race and with that true advancement carry much of the creation beside you in the world, with you.

Relationship implies the separateness of the things which are related to each other. This separation is precisely the illusion of the world that you need to understand. 'All is One' is a phrase so oft repeated that it trips off the tongue, but the implications of this phrase, when understood, shake the foundations of your personal and social worlds.

Oneness is the fundamental Truth, but knowing that Truth in all its potential is what we have termed 'Life'. It is the 'journey' of all that exists seemingly separately yet not, since all is One. In the effort to understand Oneness words are woefully superficial. Only deep contemplation will render up the secrets of Oneness to the seeker, so use our words, not to supply you the answers, but to prompt the direction of your internal ponderings so that as you explore the implications of these words their real meaning can reveal itself to you, and understanding come, not just in theory but in the inner sensing of all that surrounds you, be it object, thought, person or any other form or apparently formless aspect of experience you feel as 'Life'.

Do you sit now in a chair as you read? What is the nature and substance of the chair whereon you sit to read? A solid thing that holds your body momentarily? Of course it is, and to deny its solidity is foolish for that is indeed a fact, at one level of knowing. But ponder on the space between the atoms of the chair and it seems not so solid. Take your mind between those spaces and a whole new universe opens up to you. But further still, do those atoms not have within them whirling parts moved by what can be broadly called the 'electricity' of the universe? Is it not this charge, this energy, which holds these whirling parts in right place to each other? And is not the holding of one thing in position vis a vis another, relationship? So behind physical relationship is 'electricity,' or better described, 'energy'.

Right relationship springs from a recognition of each 'thing's' partnering relationship with other parts of the whole. To think on the Oneness of that which you call God, is to discover right relationship. Have we not said, how can something truly *be* that is not of God, since God is all there is? The unfoldment you see, the gradual awakening of the lower aspects of self to its higher source or cause, is simply a process of awareness, it is not a fact of some things being God and some not-God. Herein lies the illusion for God's is an inclusive universe.

Imagine a never-ending explosion of Light and all those waves of Light produced flung far from their source, but still remaining attached to it, and you have a graphic representation of the movement of God—each wave of light apparently journeying, yet remaining a wave of the source and eventually returning to its source. Does not respect for all things come from an understanding of this unity, that the Light, the life and power in each of those waves is the same Light whether it be shaped as a person or tree, a butterfly or a star? It is the same Light, that is why each of you in your realisation of who you truly are, *is* the Light of the world, and as you leave behind the outermost extension of you, withdrawing the lower consciousness as something no longer useful, you travel back along the wave of light that is you, and so your light increases as it returns towards its source.

So difficult it is to speak of unity with separative words! In Truth there is not you *and* the Light but only the Light which *is* you. Ponder at every opportunity this fact and all your life will change for you, all of creation become real for you and separation disappear for you. The mind of man must complicate the game, thinking in a linear fashion of that which is non-linear but whole, simultaneous, and does not in truth move because it is One. What appears as movement is simply the ripple of awareness of itself and what we call manifestation is the farthest extension of that awareness into a certain kind of possibility—materiality.

How non-sensical are your social divisions when seen in the Light of Truth! When your aim is not to divide through privilege and status, possession and cultural distinction, but to uplift the consciousness of each to awareness that each is Light, how fast would all the 'problems' of your world disappear and the Earth reap only benefit from thee. Not in weakness, in caving in to the demands of power and separative thinking will this golden era come, but through the absolute strength of those that know themselves to be of Light; not in imposition of their will on others, but in their example, and in their staying in the Truth of who they are and by that Truth acknowledging the Truth in others; discerning social games from Truth, pride from strength of Will, and Love from desire.

Around and through all these topics this book will move, that you may learn to recognise by which intent you set your relationships to stand; through which eye you see the world. This is not a vision imposed on others, for the spiritual master is master of himself. He does not recruit, nor force himself on others, but accepts with Love those who come to him to learn. But the learning is theirs, and for it they alone are responsible. The master's responsibility is to ensure the purity of his own intent as it is the pupil's to purify his intent.

Always in these books we have come back to the intent, for the quality of intent brings you the quality of your experience, and only honest examination of intent will reveal the reasons for your 'failures' and 'successes' to you. There is no real failure or success in the unity of God, only realisation, and it is the quality of your realisation with which we are concerned.

Read on, friends. Wander through these pages, not in effort to understand, but to allow understanding to be effortless, as the functions of a healthy body are effortless. With greater understanding your intent will alter, and so your life be shaped by that which is higher, and the Light which is you be realised and known, and its purity and brightness shape your intent.

The Two Worlds

Relationship is at the heart of all the problems of man. If he realised this, the path to their unravelling would become clearer to him. It seems to man a complex web, sticky with difficulty, clouded by issues and doubt, that to progress he must walk some thin strand of achievability, or rest in the thick cushion of his latest comfort zone. Change your view and the reality will change for you. These clinging, sticky webs of the astral world do not have to be reality for you. They are the cloudy shrouds built by the doubts, fears, hopes and desires of you, and all who 'live' in the world beside you. They catch you in a static world of past action, past hurt, past deprivation, past hope and past wantings. They are the astral substance which hides the Light of his soul from man.

Your soul stands in a different world, overlaid, yet penetrating if allowed, this misted astral world of humanity. The world of the soul is a world of clarity and Light. It moves in sparkling spirals, cutting through those webs as if they were not there. In fact it knows them not. Think on the difference between these worlds and you will know in which you wish to remain and which you wish to pursue. The world of the soul funnels its light into the personal body of you. It arrives as clarity but your own barriers determine the measure and colour of what is left for you to use. When you lift your consciousness beyond the sticky webs of doubt and cloudy issues, the funnelled stream, this energy of Light can enter in and gradually the fogs of delusion—stripped—dissolve about you, and the Light of the soul stands at last on Earth, shining, revealed in you.

How many moments of your day are truly free of doubt, negativity or other of the multifarious aspects of fear? How many times a day do you fear for some kind of loss or find yourself in mental or emotional struggle. Such things may seem to be the nature of man, but why? Is effort always accompanied by pain of one sort or another? Happy indeed is the one who can expend effort without anguish and see with clarity what is rightfully his path and be clear as to the quality of his intent.

Do not blame the world for the state of your life, and likewise do not blame yourself for the state of the world. The Truth behind the world does not depend upon your perception of it, but your experience is bound to your perception. It follows then that the more you live in the Light of your soul the greater will be the change in your perception of what you call 'the world'. What constitutes this world for you?

The world of materiality, as we have said, is at the farthest reaches of each wave. Thus it is a journey into density, and the journey back to the source, one of expansion. As the wave concentrates, its density or physicality increases. Because it is the density that you see and experience in your world, the light that is the wave is less apparent. When you learn to place your attention higher along the wave, closer to its source, the light of the wave becomes more apparent or 'visible' to you and you see how all that is, is infused with it because in the end, light is what it actually is. The light then, is always available to you. What you see is more a matter of choice than you realise. It depends entirely on where you choose to stand to view, and your capability of staying on that point. Remember this when judging the view of others.

You would not blame a blind man for not being able to see the world the sighted see, would you? Do not therefore blame the unenlightened for the darkness of their view.

There is in the end no rightness or wrongness to any expression of being except in relation to a purpose or aim, then all that can be said is that something is inappropriate or ineffective, given a particular desire or aim. Let us explain. A beautiful flower that is produced without the ability to grow seed of itself is not wrong or a failure, except if the aim of its production was to provide for its perpetuation. Obviously, a flower without seed cannot perpetuate itself. But only in relation to this goal is the flower 'wrong'.

What you do cannot therefore ever be said to be wrong except in relation to a desired aim, and this you would do well to remember in your forming opinions of others. Herein lies the 'freedom' of creation. Yet this freedom is not perhaps freedom after all as each is subject to the Law—the constraints of cause and effect—and the limits of the thought that sent that wave of Creation forth. But that which creates the thought itself is free to choose, according to its nature, from the infinite potential that God *is*. So the apparent paradoxes of existence begin, a mind free to create, but bound in the effects it can create by the nature (the quality) of its intent; the physical being bound by the 'laws' of physicality, yet its operating consciousness being free to govern that physicality or its experience of that physicality from any vantage point along the wave of its creation.

The paradoxes and confusions arise when you begin to move your own attention from the purely physical view further up the wave, from where, suddenly, you can see both what has been known and thought of as fixed, and what is less tangible, more fluid—the wave springing from a thought which can be reshaped and directed anew by the changing of intent and the mastery of a higher point of view. We speak of higher because it is closer to the source and therefore of greater power, closer to the cause than to effect. You are as a branch in a multitude of waves effecting everything from your higher point of consciousness up those waves.

When you see all that you do as part of a unity, and when you understand rightly your unalterable connection to everything else that is the whole you call God, loneliness, depression, frustration, anger and any other form of separateness departs from you. Oneness is not an ideal, but a fact, and it is only realisation that bars this fact from you. When you feel, in every body of your being, that you are joined inextricably to all of Creation that stands on all the worlds beside you, the might and comfort of God infuses you, and no apparent evil, in desiring opposition to that unity can tear this Godliness from you. In knowledge of such unity there is no pride or little superiority of personality, no glamour to eat like cancer the Love of all from out inside of you, for once cemented, this experience of unity holds firm, suffices you. You cannot walk in doubt when each step is supported, cannot suffer despair when each moment is held in Love surrounding you.

Concentrate on unity and each contemplation on the Truth supports you with the rest, for one aspect of the whole must give you all the rest. When Truth is grasped, even evil can be understood and lay no claim on you. You accept another's choice, and realisation of eternal Good ousts the black temptation from your mind, and evil, which attempts through opposition to impose disunity on you, is seen as an unsustainable idea which cannot forever depart its universal home where Love, Will and Wisdom hold the reality of relationship in their One hand.

He who is at peace with himself is at peace with the 'world'. Each of you *is* your world as truly as I AM all there is in the world, yet what you see in the world is not Me, but the imaginings of Me; the apparent movement of all that lies in the void as it springs out on waves of Light, creating time, distance, space—attributes of My imagining that exist only in so far as they are sensed by those aspects of Me that place their consciousness in receptivity to the waves of Light imagined by Me. How can this be? If I AM Stillness and everything that seems to move is simply My thought 'creating' wave patterns of many universes, then sensation on any plane is simply the vibration of one wave resonating on another. Do you see then that these waves are products, sensations of Me, yet are not Me except in so far as I AM their source. Are the waves emitted by a radio the radio itself? If you would know the radio, would you not examine the radio and not its waves? So then, seek Me not in the sensations of the worlds, for all you will find will be an endless entertainment.

If you would know the flower, seek not its appearance, but the essence of Me from which it springs. My ideas spring forth in greater and greater particularity the 'further' their wave 'travels' from Me, and so you will find in the flower of your garden merely the echo of the splendor that sent it forth. And travelling back with your consciousness from that echo to its source, you will discover beings—devas—the greater embodiment of the flower as they are closer to the beginning of the flower's waveform that has sprung as a thought from Me.

Do you not see then why all that I have created is sacred to Me? And so too it should be sacred to thee. What gentleness would rule the Earth if all realised that each atom beside them in the world originates with Me, and what freedom would there be in realising that the being of those atoms lies not in their physicality at all, but in the Stillness of Me, and knowledge of them can only be truly found in acquaintance with Me, for they are nothing and I AM everything.

The fragile mind of man cannot know full the glory of Me, any more than a particle of dust can stay where it sits in face of a blasting wind. Humanness is merely a fragment of your being, so if you would experience the glory of knowing Me, you must travel back along your light wave bungy cord

of sensate being until you behold more and more the lightness
and greatness of Me.

Sit in stillness and know that in every cell of your body
I AM. Sit in stillness and know that every space between
your atoms contains Me for they *are* not except that they
are contained in Me. Such power you will have, when you
work not with descriptions of the world but with the essence
of what has produced the world. If you would know how
to create that which is in harmony with the Earth, feel the
essence of its being, and in this you will come closer to its
essence in Me.

All that you approach in reverence as an aspect of Me
shall render up to you its part in the nature of Me, and
you shall find your way out of the chaos of your sensory
world and into the everlasting completeness of Me. For I
am complete and My completion is the answer to all of
your woes. How can there be lack when all the possibility
there can be is contained within thee, not in finding, for
it moves not, not in seeing, for I cannot be sensed, but I
can be known. Whatever you think you are, you are not,
for everything that can be seen, heard or sensed about you
is just an idea dancing around My universe of ideas. If
you would know who you are you must know Me, and all
things that I *seem* to be are One thing, and all is contained
in each thing as it is contained in Me.

If the movement of the universe is illusory, how can
attending to any part of the waveform lead to Truth when
that waveform is itself illusory? What we are discussing here is
awareness. Because you think now that the imaginary journey
of your incarnations is the reality, you must begin where you
are, since you cannot adequately perceive anything else. Only
a receptive consciousness can turn one's awareness from *where*
it thinks it is and *what* it thinks it is, to contemplating, looking
for, and eventually comprehending the Reality of Truth.
Remember it is a part of Me that has made the journey you

think is your journey and thus you think yourself separate from Me.

In Truth, full awareness cannot 'destroy' you since you are Me, but such is the 'distance' of your thought from Me that exposure to too great a Light of My power would sever for uncountable ages more, your tiny consciousness from Me. Yet such threat is not real for I do not attack Myself. My creations, however, are free to war with each other or be at peace. They have My power to become whatever they imagine themselves to be, yet they remain imaginings until they return to the Reality of Me.

Thus it is, time after time, as you journey off in apparent independence from Me, you become incarnate, extending your wave to the slow reaches of materiality, playing your games, forgetting My name. Hark then, if you would escape from the endless wheel of your becomings. Turn deliberately to face Me and govern the materiality of thee with the Light of Me as that Light is manifest through the soul of thee. And when each fibre of your physical, emotional and mental being is infused with and directed by My Light, then the Light will in fact walk the Earth with thee, and all that comes into contact with thee will be lit and raised through the grace of Me as I shine through thee.

Death need take you not unless you let it, and mastery of even this is yours when your creations, even as your body is a creation of thine, are fully commanded by the highest aspects of thee. Would you return to Me, even thy soul must in the end be 'sacrificed' to the Light that I AM, and incomprehensible is the bliss that awaits the soul returning to Me.

There are many paths to the One, it has been said, and this is true for is there not an infinitude to My imaginings? Why are you so afraid of My joy? Like a child you are, who, discovering a flame, wants to make a bonfire on a dry, grassy plain. Soon he finds himself surrounded by flame, and knows not that he imagined both fire and flame. It is the untainted trust of the innocent child that you must bring to your questing for Me, and purity of a harmless heart is what will render My Love and My Power to thee. Turn your face from the destroying flame and discover the fire that drives My universe does not burn.

Darkness & Light

The void: a velvety blackness that issues no light; so deep it is stillness where nothing is, its embrace as comforting as anything bright. Forget about evil a moment for 'knowledge' of evil has robbed you of Life, and if you would know Me, you must know My blackness as well as My Light. All that *is* awaits in it, comfortable, unseparated and therefore complete.

I have said Darkness and Light are the faces of Me, but is this right? For really My Darkness is actually Light. Be comfortable with My Darkness and you will find it is Light. They are the same thing, for I AM One. In the void are the mountains and any manifested 'thing' resides there in the darkness with them. When you stand before the reality of My mountains, blackness may seem to stand behind you, for the blackness contains them and it is merely the shape of the potential of them in the blackness that is reflected in Light.

In the stillness of Me, I think and My imagining ripples as does a wave upon the sea. Sound is My wave, singing out of My void, singing angels, singing worlds, and thee. The sound of My wave creates Light from My Darkness appearing as night, and appearing as day for all Creation sings the tunes the Piper plays.

Be not afraid of My Darkness. There is no evil here. It will wrap you in My stillness and you will find peace here. How can I in Truth be divided into Darkness and Light?

I AM both together, at the same 'time' and when you find your home in My Darkness, My Light will blaze forth from you in measure greater than a universe of suns for you will be not separated from those suns.

The duality of your worlds is but an imitation, a reflection of the simultaneous Darkness and Lightness of Me. Your minds cannot but for an instant glimpse them as one. So the things of the night are hid from you and under cover of this false darkness which lacks understanding of Me, evil deeds are hid and ignorance and denial of My omnipresence keeps you from true knowledge and comfort of both My night and My day.

Your worlds are but a reflection on the consciousness of your minds. How will your experience be clear if the pool of your mind in which you see it is ruffled and unstill? The strength of your emotions are as a breeze or a hurricane across this pool. You will never see the mountains if the pool is never still and deep. This is why My blackness is still for by its stillness the brilliance of what I AM can shine forth and from its depth the infinitude that I AM can come forth.

Between the depth of Me and the Light of Me you have erected your pool—the emotions, the feelings, the thinking and expectations which govern what you think is your life—stand as a barrier between you and Me. Only when you abandon these inventions do you see Me. Only when your pool is still and open to the sky will you see me, and when you cover it with storm clouds or apparitions of your own making you will see only your own inventions, not Me. All the activity of your world is like a breeze that ripples the pond for thee, so take time out from activity to still the pond that you might see Me.

Remove yourself from the doorway of fear to truly know the Darkness of Me wherein I AM One and Darkness and Light are that Oneness of Me. Let my warm, inky blackness comfort thee. Let its stillness rest and nurture thee, then will My Light shine brightest in thee for all that sits there with thee, to see.

From where man stands it seems to him that what he sees, the 'solidity' of the world is real, yet in fact there are more spaces in the world than there are those points of solidity on which his perception of the world depends. These spaces are the physical expression of the black velvet spaces wherein lies God's potential. You cannot, with your physical eyes, see those spaces but you can enter with your mind. And think not that all you do with your mind 'unreal'. It is your link to the Truth as well as the mechanism by which you manufacture the false.

Your power over the physical dwells in the spaces between those points that are visible. It is here that mind truly resides and because of the power inherent in these velvety spaces you are afraid to know this night for you deem it the province of the dark forces that would, if they could, take all the power of the Light. But naught can in Truth oppose what God is, and in the end all must return to that Truth and reside in the expanding peace of God again. Give no power to evil and it cannot assail you.

Stray not from your intent to know all as an expression of God. Learn and understand the Law of God—His key that mirrors your intent—and ruthlessly recognise that which is of your personality and that which is of your soul intent. When the personality seeks only direction of the soul and higher Self (that divinity of you that sits 'above' your soul), harm cannot enter in. Even if by some error it does, seek not to punish yourself but to quickly correct the *motive* of your intent. Be vigilant, for many are the seductions of the glamorous distractions that masquerade as good which actually feed the puffed-up ego of the personality's intent. To be a true servant of divinity should be your intent.

In the still, velvet blackness of God's night lies the determination of the fruitfulness of your intent, for here is your peace and certainty, and from this springs forth in Light that which lies in potential, hid. Although all that can be lies in it, it is by nature private—your own security of place in the depths of God. Your rest, your peace and your deep consideration of 'how' to proceed is here. Remember it is the spaces that contain the world and for every right knowing you have of these spaces there springs forth a light.

The void is at once an ocean, a space. Dive into the space and you will find the fire. Find the fire and you will find Earth, solidified. These things are all from My One thing, all ideas in the perfection of the One idea. Be still that the void shall be known to you.

How can this be? Remember God moves not, and movement comes from the illusion that what is One is divided. That illusion is your inability to see that what lies hid in still blackness *is* Light. No logic of concrete mind will answer this mystery for you. It must be pondered, meditated, experienced, to be grasped and if, in the contemplation of these writings you have found it not, then let what here is written point the way.

Detachment

Grief is, like all other strong emotions, a result of human perception. Since divinity is the only thing which is both real and permanent, grief for anything lost is grief for that which was neither real nor permanent to begin with. To grieve for that which is no longer present in your life is to look backwards, to desire the outer form over the inner reality. If you would remove grief and loss from your life, move your perception to that which is present—the Love, glory and Reality of divinity and all that is discernibly divine.

Each aspect of divinity has its own path of expression. The human path can in one respect be described as evolutionary—to travel 'forward' to greater and greater realisation of the Light of divinity. Not all that has been in the world beside you has been on this path, for some have been on the path of involution. For you involution is a looking backwards and cannot but bring you sorrow and helplessness if you indulge in its perception. Grief is of necessity a looking backwards, a wanting for that which was, a confusion on your part and a dwelling on involution.

Those who can remove themselves from the physical reality to the realisation of the more evolved planes of higher evolution, know that for which others grieve, either as an illusion best forgotten or as an aspect of divinity that dies not, but stands always in Creation beside them. And what is Creation? Creation is the bringing forth as perception by the thinker of all the potential that God is, of all the potential that lies in the so-called void. The void is that velvet blackness of deep night from whence arises all that can possibly be, from the mountains of Earth to the flowers of many planets, the tiniest grain of sand and the sound of angels that gathers molecules together to make water, that gathers the powers of the unseen air to make wind. None of these things can *be* without potential, and understanding of potential is the secret to your steady evolution.

In the experiencing of your world you are seeing only a tiny fragment of the potential there is, the passing fragmented end of a long chain of expressions 'to be'. The instant your perception moves from the physical end result of being to an understanding and awareness of the permanence of the divinity behind the physical being, you begin to comprehend the Reality of Being, and know that which is behind the physical reality. Then can you begin to realise that what you grieved for in loss never truly was, but its divinity, the Truth of its being, never ceases to be.

Sentiment is akin to grief and neither are truly Love, but are human longing and desire manufactured by the personality. If these seem harsh words, let us explain thus: Love, as God Loves, gives ever outwards. Grief and sentiment pull in, trying to hold something to the small self. They support nothing whereas Love supports everything.

Being of God, Love is the structure and support of the universe. It addresses the need of the moment and being appropriate to the human path evolves your understanding to the next level. Grief, sentiment and such emotions look backwards and involve you in what has been. This inward, backward movement is, as we have said, not evolution but involution. Love—as God loves—put into daily practise, being structural, outgoing, the solidity that God *is*, must support you at times and circumstances when others wallow in despair and the human 'condition' renders their circumstance quicksand.

Love, as God loves, is not a thing of the past or the future, it is of now, but only by detachment from the perils of human emotion can you experience Love.

Compassion is the child of true Love, not pity, sympathy or hope. None of these elevates the human being to a place of detachment from the causes of suffering. Compassion on the other hand is a recognition of struggle and the offering of the solid hand of Love, not to rescue, for how can there be 'rescue' from illusion? There can only be recognition of error, of a view taken that was 'true' for the human fabrication, but not true for the Reality in which is God, the divinity that is behind and intrinsic to all of you in Truth.

Each moment you are faced with choice; to join the illusion of the world of human emotion, or to live in the Truth. A few minutes practice every hour, in identification with God's Love, will find you quickly learning how to be a conduit for that Love, changing your life from a negative receptor of worldly strife to a positive generator of true Life.

Ponder often on the nature of God's Love, not as it has been interpreted by men and women of the past, by religious or other social institutions, but as you have discovered it to be in the deepest reaches of your soul in moments of surety when you know yourself to be God, when no separation stands between God's all inclusive Love and you who are also of that Love, when you can feel it pouring from the eternal generator that comes from way inside you yet is also from above you. It pours through you and all that occupy the heavenly planes with you, whether lying in apparent acquiescence in the deep night of God or in the manifested Light that is the true structure built of the true substance of the universe.

True Love, because it is of God, builds. It always *is*, and while standing in its presence, questions plaguing the life of temporality do not exist. In your world you constantly 'see' 'things' or circumstances replaced by other 'things'. In the stream that is God's Love, replacement is an irrelevancy that enters not into the question. In fact God's Love, being complete, contains no questions. This is why it has oft been said to be the answer to all your questions. How hard it must be to understand for those who have never stood recipient and generator of its path!

Alignment

In the language of words, alignment means to line several things up with each other sequentially. This is misleading when 'alignment' is used to describe an act essential to your increase in spiritual awareness.

Although in Reality you are a unity that exists only in that which we call God, your present consciousness is centred in the outer end of your extension from His imagining, as we have described. It is because of this state of your consciousness that we must talk first in separative words, about apparently distinct parts of you that you need to 'align'. First you must understand what you have done in your imagining yourself to be separate from the unity of God *is*. Only then you can begin to correct this erroneous separative thinking and alter the reality that you experience.

Your emotions, your intellect, your physical body, and your spiritual consciousness are in your mind segmented, and thus you dive from one to the other in your daily experience. If you would realise the 'kingdom of heaven,' you must bring these divergent parts of your mind's thinking into alignment, melding them under the control of that which is higher than these lower aspects of yourself that you think are you.

You are like tops that wobble off centre, and if you would spin like a perfectly balanced top, you must gather all your power to your centre. When your consciousness is centred, you do not have to struggle to monitor your emotions, your intellect or your physical body. Those apparently separate aspects of you will obey, for they will be merged into one unified consciousness that is the true expression of your being manifesting on the physical plane.

All our wordy explanations of relationship, of power, love, intelligence, and the many views of the same subject we have presented in these books for you, are given that you might understand. And when understanding is gained, it can be abandoned, as all the separate learnings you were taught—in how to drive a car or do up the laces of your shoes—are abandoned when the learning is done, and the execution becomes a smooth, unified action that requires no examination of its parts. And so the command of your lower bodies must become for you. Learn, learn, and understand, and practise the commanding of emotions, intellect, and physical body in Light of our teachings to you, and 'alignment' will automatically become reality for you. Is that not mastery?

No one commands the pattern of waveforms that you are except you, and no influence can enter into your mind unless you let it. You are told to be vigilant, but vigilance is not required when you learn to place all your energies in the service of the highest aspects of you. Then will you feel the flow of Life across your bridge, in through the head centres, and through the subtle and physical bodies that you see as you. It takes no effort. In fact, it is effort that prevents its flow through you. Did we not say, at the beginning, that revelation comes, not with effort, but in the suspension of effort?

For mankind now, Love is the great aligning force. The task now is to infuse all that manifests as physicality, with Love. It is the binding aspect of Me, and thus it fuses what appears to be separate. With the organising attribute of Intelligence, and the uniting attribute of Love, all can

then be brought under the direction of Will. Do you see
then, how in your own life you must embrace and submit
to Love before you can wield the power that as part of Me
is your right to wield? Align then first with Love and your
asking for power shall sit aright.

Study Love, not as man sees it, which is merely desire,
but as God *is* it; all embracing, unifying, non-excluding,
a gentleness that is a strength unsurpassed. It waivers not
and seeks the highest good. You find it so hard to realise
that truly Love is power, yet it never harms, never justifies
a means by an end. Truly, Love obliterates all appearances
of wrong. But if you would have it, you must turn aside
from your own rightness of petty opinion, no matter how
legitimately you feel that opinion was gained.

The strength of divine Love does not live in your
personality, but in divinity itself, and it is to divinity you
must turn when seeking to know Love. Then will you find it
moving outwards from inside of you. Love never crushes the
aspirations of others but raises those aspirations to a higher
good. But do not try to send Love to those actively engaged
in evil that *they think* can destroy Love. Instead, establish
Love first inside yourself, so that your own bastion of Love
is unassailable. Ask Love, not your personality or intellect,
what use to make of Love. Withhold it not, but neither force
it on those hostile to its being, for such an act is not Love but
imposition of personal will. Love does not force, it just *is*.
Love is always available and need not be sought. Alignment
then, is the bringing of all your separate intents into the unity
of Love, so that all your desires meet in your heart. Alignment
could be described also as intelligent submission.

It is the essence of Being that Love accepts uncondition-
ally, not a behaviour of that being's extension in the world
of echoes. Life is yours forever. It does not rely on your
goodness. The criminal and the saint equally have life in
Me. Behaviour creates its own rewards not for the act but

through the quality of purpose behind the act. You cannot judge therefore, from your worldly point of view, what is punishment for whom.

If Love is the glue that builds My ideas into creations, can My creations be destroyed? Yes and no. No, because all My ideas remain with Me for I move not and nothing can be lost from Me for I AM all that is, and loss of My creations is but an illusion. The movement you think is creation is merely the waves of My thinking and nothing is created in Truth that does not already lie acquiescent in Me as the totality that I AM. Yes, because that which Love binds together is bound through the direction of Will and Will can equally redirect, and that which is seemingly created be re-created or rather re-formed as seemingly something else. Thus it seems to you that I destroy. Everything around you is infused with My Light. My Light surrounds you in the Earth, in space, in the stars. The universe *is* not, without My Light. You need only move your consciousness a little to be conscious of My Light.

Allow My energy to flow through you. You do not have to initiate anything. When you step your own will aside you allow the Will of the higher Life to drive your physical experience. You have become afraid of allowing, thinking that every step, every movement has to be initiated. Once the channels are open between the higher and lower aspects of your being you need not initiate acts of will. In fact it is better you do not. The Will of your soul has impetus enough for any activity in your physical plane life. Why, once the way is opened, would you want to deny the higher flow and keep substituting instead the lesser view? Does this not create tension and barriers for you, crystallising eventually in your body and jamming the circuitry of mind?

When you stay in the connection of your soul and let it become governor and initiator of your physical form life, the qualities of your heart too will find a place there, slipping in where choice has gone, and heart (Love) and Will become a partnership and work as one.

Such plenitude presupposes that you already know how to let your mind be lit by the Light of your soul, that your intent is always focused on the higher, and you can register in the body, personality and mind of your lower being, the impulse and breath of your soul. A hurdle indeed this may seem to those unpractised in these themes. Yet daily diligence and focus of the heart and mind will bring these things, and swiftly at last your footsteps will find themselves along the path. Work with Me, not despite Me. The obstacles of your life dissolve away.

Worry not, for worry is a fixation on form and if you live rightly, form is known as the outcome of energy and thought. It flows naturally as a consequence and requires only that once the techniques of physical manipulation are automatic (as in driving a car), you need pay attention only to the light of intent that flows in easy rivers from Life itself. Of this Life is not your Self a vital part? This does not mean you do nothing, but that your busyness is not driven by social requirements. How much that is driven by social convention do you think is the choice of your soul? Let your busyness serve the greater Life, which of course is represented by your fellow man and by the beings inhabiting the universe with you, from ants to streams to planets, space and suns. All are filled with Life and within Life each must serve the other. Think on this.

That which is lower must serve the higher, but does not the higher—just by being what it is—serve the lower? This symbiosis does not depend on their awareness of each other, but awareness speeds the journey of mindfulness and the one who is more mindful carries with them greater parts of the rest. Thus to raise the consciousness of others is both a consequence and necessity of your own rising, but carries with it the greater and greater responsibility of the rest. How could you face this responsibility with only the personality to act or guide you? How could you trust this puny, shifting vehicle with the responsibility of the rest? But what magnificence can be achieved by the one who centres his life in the soul and then, as the masters have done, given even this glory away for the higher glory of divine Will and allowed that greater Light to drive the thoughts and actions of their work and play.

When we sit in prayer we sit in humbleness at the glory of God's welcome. Do not think, My children, that you pray alone, for how can you be alone when God is all the Creation that sits beside you and your state of being affects all states of being and therefore all that *is* 'hears' your prayer.

Constance is a virtue sought by many and ever the difficult question of man is how to attain constance when moving seems to be the state of living. Constance is the stillness of the steady heart from which life can be lived in true glory and acknowledgment of God's presence. Constance is the rock we spoke of, upon which your soul unmoving anchors. Constance occurs when all the subtle and physical bodies of your being are aligned to your nature and purpose, when naught of small delay or petty concern knocks any body off its place at centre.

That which comes from God belongs to God and to be all that one can be is to know the origin of one's being. To hear the angels speak one must know one is an angel, and angels sing because they must. To be and not express that being is an impossibility within the thought of God. Take care therefore, that the existent being of yourself is never far from the thought of God itself.

Nothing shakes your permanent and unbreakable link to Me. Only *perception* of the wavering and doubts of personality can seeming shake this unbreakable connection to Me, for you form an unending chain of being from your divine Self to the multitudinous expressions that are 'you'. It is merely the aspect or appearance of these aspects of your self that seems to change. To know always the permanent, unassailable nature of your link to God, which is not a link but an extension or continuation of God, is to allow perfect freedom in all your bodies for all move then on the fulcrum of total trust and silence that spins in gloried singing to every plane and universe on which God makes expression.

Sense & Knowledge

Love is the attribute of God that is Oneness, for how can that which binds not be Oneness when it is an essential characteristic that makes God what God is? Love is God's glue. But wait, is this not a world of opposites that you inhabit? Night, day, dark, light, male, female, hot, cold. Did we not say that relationship is both the reality and illusion of the world? To create movement out of Oneness, the One imagines each of its possibilities as a pair of 'opposites' that are constantly moving alternately towards and away from each other. Thus the Light that is the wave has its characteristic form.

It is the wave action itself that is the illusion. The original potentiality—from which it sprang as thought—remains, unformed and unalterable in the Oneness we call God. It can be said to be the substance of God in which all His ideas rest, and which changes not and moves not. The ideas we have called Intelligence are the potential of all possibility that rests forever acquiescent in the Stillness that God is. It is God's Will or power that enables the imagining of God to be, and it is Will by which all the potentiality that is God *is*.

From your perspective then, it could be said that creation of the worlds grows from the apparent splitting of substance into moving complements through the power of Will and the binding attribute of Love. Love, however, seems not to apply, else how can the opposites be opposites? But the wave is an appearance, formed of imagining, and as extensions of God, you too have the power of imagining. So, though the Life behind your life changes not, your individual lives are controlled by your own imaginings, though in Reality you reside in Stillness, as a potential of God.

Here, at the farthest extent of your imagining, you seem to be composed of dualities, where the pure colours of God are polarised into many and the pure sounds of God seem to compete for supremacy. There is no disharmony in God, and if you would live in a world of harmony, you need only cease your own imaginings and leave the imagining to God. The higher up your chain of command you go, the closer you will be to the experience of God's harmony. And you will find, paradoxically, that by staying closer in consciousness to your source in God, that you will create, but your creations will be harmonious.

'The flowers smell divine,' you say, but what is it that smells and who is it that smells it? The world of the body in which you dwell is a world of senses, all electrical impressions of waveforms of Light upon one another. The waveform of the flower resonates, and the waveform of your physicality is receptive to those vibrations. All your world is, is an uncounted complexity of waveforms resonating to each other. Some feel harmonious to you and some do not. Your body and particularly your brain, merely stores these resonance impressions within their own waves, and until they are released to return to the Stillness from which they sprang, they remain as part of what you think is you.

We will not say that these waveforms are not you, for all practical purposes, you are where your consciousness rests. But if you would experience the potential of what you are, attend well to this. You are an idea in the mind of God. You are not God, rather God is playing at being you.

You can go on forever, describing, experiencing the waveforms that are the imaginings of God, and such a pursuit will, as we have said, keep you well entertained. But the power is not in the watching of the movie, but in the making of it, and if you would direct your own movie with full consciousness, you must learn the difference between the vibrations of the waveforms and knowledge of the idea that sent them forth. Every moment of the day, humans give their power away, thinking themselves to be merely a player in this greatest of plays.

Fabricate not your life from the recordings of your senses, from submission to those echoes of God's Light waves. Know instead that you are still, in all power as part of Him, and knowledge of His ideas will gift you the power of creation. What you know in God must bring you the production from that knowledge as a waveform you experience.

Stop in the busyness of your days to hear what song My universe plays and depart your attention from that which your ego-driven personality has come to want to play. Sound *is* the energy of your thought, forming not only your words but your world. Silence can be the gold of well-directed thought where others might speak their boulders larger with each utterance not brought to soul-conscious thought first.

When we sing the night, we are the night. The two energies (ours and the night) are one and thus are we refreshed. To sing an energy is to identify with it, to become that which is sung, and upon which our consciousness dwells. This is the secret all the Ancients know for healing, health and the purification of the body to receive the soul. The sound is discovered in the identification. The two processes are one. Since you are also sound, the purity of your sound or otherwise builds life or boulders—allows the stream of divine consciousness to pass unhindered or diverts the channelled flow until the consciousness is lost and down the rivers of discomfort thy life does flow. To identify with the night is to enjoin with it, and thus to enjoy its being. It needs not that you dance naked under the stars but in the nakedness of your soul, for is not the realised soul naked of deceit?

What is the sound of a healthy body part? Does not the golden rod of the spine have a sound? And does not the perversion of its sound cause hurt? What is the sound of alignment? A gentle click or a mighty hum? Both, for alignment may be the tiniest movement away and yet release the mightiest power.

Would not that which is constructed of right sound and aligned to the sound of the Cosmos be both a generator and an amplifier of sound? And that which embodies Truth must be all things at once together, both process and product—the One and at the same time the many—in a mirrored process that cannot be comprehended by the attention focused only on one aspect of the many, seeing not both process and stillness, source and product. Separation falls out of perception and unity-born experience dissolves argument of form, without negation.

Seek not the pleasure of the senses but the idea from which they spring. Knowledge of the flower will give you both flower and experience of this beautiful thing. Knowing sits with God and where but in God do you really dwell? Knowing is never in the future, but always now. It waits not for time, for time it knows nothing of. Whatever you have in your mind in the instant you truly know it, it *is*. So, if you would keep your heart's greatest desires, you must know them, through every hour.

When you know fear, it will come to you. When you know hate, it will arrive on your doorstep, and when you know Love, it will support you as its wings support the dove. Do not wish then to be something, but *know* it is what you are. Knowing places you in God and longing dangles you about in wasted hope. Waste not a moment in hoping for things for hope but echoes a passing flicker, a pointless desire that flies past your eyes. Knowledge is as firm as God, based deep within the depth of you. Wavering not, it is Creation's core, the gift of God that you hold with you, now and forever.

Divine Reason

It is time for man to understand the true nature of his being. Human being is but a tiny part of your being. It is just a feeler you have put out to experience in a different way. You exist on all levels of consciousness and at all stages of development simultaneously.

Time, a grand illusion of your level of consciousness is not a reality of higher planes where it is realised that all the potential that God is, exists simultaneously, because God is a totality, a unity, and though the ideas of God may seem to manifest sequentially, they are nonetheless simultaneously contained within, not separate from, their Creator. Neither can they be separate from each other.

What you do now, what you think this moment therefore, ripples simultaneously through all your past and future experiences, because it is only your attending consciousness that experiences a 'reality'. The wordy explanations of man are full of paradoxes when speaking of Truth. In the 'language' of divine reason, no such paradox is evidenced because it *is* the simplicity of Truth.

If divine reason has form, then that form is Light and such Light is not described, but comprehended. That is why the wise speak seldom, knowing that the pollution of words may distort the Light of reason and prevent the seeker from finding Truth. If you are not sure, then you have not reasoned divinely, yet Truth is never fanatical, it just *is*. In the maelstrom of your world, Truth must be sought in Silence until you take the Silence with you into the melee of the world.

Whether your life now be wealthy or poor, healthy or unwell, it is a result of a stand of consciousness, and a change of stance can render all present conditions void. It is from the void that you choose which reality to suffer or enjoy. But if your choice is governed not by divine reason, but by the little self, then will you choose suffering over glory and pain over joy. A master is one who has learned to reason divinely. All his choices have been made for the highest good, and not one creation of God is invalidated by his choice.

What is divine reason? To reason is to reach for the Truth, to sit in a world of effects and discover their cause. You should wonder, if you have thought about it at all, how you can recognise Truth when you are caught in a consciousness that listens to the echoes of My thought, that thinks the waveforms of My imaginings are the Reality that I AM. Intellectual reason is based on premises and systems of logic built to examine, yay even in minute detail, these echoes of Me. In man, but not in man alone, the creative ability of what I AM extends and distorts the waves emanating from Me, and constructs both in and out of harmony with the Reality that I AM.

Divine reason rests not on premises or logic, though these may assist you to discover divine reason. Nay, divine reason springs as axiomatic from the recognition and acceptance that I AM and that you also are that I AM. Divine reason can be expressed, but it cannot be taught, and each must come in his own way and time to its realisation. Realisation of the qualities of Me comes in measure of the ability to comprehend. Thus it must be that the view man has of Me will be modified as he progresses in his ability to under-stand. So caught up is man in the complex waveforms of his world of time, space and place, that he often mistakes his own projection of his mind for qualities of Me, and so he can justify anything he wishes to do in My name. If his interpretation and understanding would grow, he must abandon both his idea of man and his idea of Me. Only when you have no judgement can the heart be opened and upon pure invitation can My attributes enter in. Of these, Love is now the greatest lesson, remembering, however, that each of My attributes contains the others. For this present incarnation of your solar system, My attributes are comprehended as threefold, but in the next, this will not be so, for the understanding then, will be a greater whole.

When you are 'thinking,' you are not reasoning divinely, for thinking is a product of knowing, and divine reason is a state of knowing. That state, however, can produce its own waves of thought and action, and because it rests in the knowing of Me, it will be right thinking and right action.

So, you cannot recognise divine reason in the multitude of waveforms that constitute your 'reality,' unless you have experienced My attributes of Love, Will and Intelligence which have been elsewhere discussed in these books. We repeat here that to have knowledge of one of My attributes, is to have access to understanding of them all since I AM not in Truth divided, but only in seeming, for the purpose of your present comprehension.

Since Love is the primary lesson of your world, let Love be your doorway to Me. Since Intelligence is the 'child' of Love and Power, and has already been infused into the substance of being on the physical plane, you need seek it not. Attend now to Love, and in so far as you are able, knowledge of Love will bring you glimpses of understanding of My Power. My Power extends to you as will, and what you express as your own will is best directed by your recognition and knowledge of My Love.

Earth & Humanity

So hard it is for beginners on the path to freedom! Diving in and out of clouds that blind you from the Light—one moment understanding and seeing what you are, the next returning to the lies of 'Earthly' existence. Weariness, illness, despair, irritation, illness and death—all things you think 'natural,' yet how unnatural can it be for that which is pure Spirit in Reality, to die, or to fall ill, suffer annoyance or loss of that Spirit of any kind?

Do not blame the Earth. You know Her not, and the magnificence of Her being but provides a stage for the kingdoms formed of her substance on which to play. Such richness and companionship the Earth has offered you. You think yourselves alone on Earth, yet a multitude of waves create the world with you. Humans are but one great wave. What of the other waves?

They all spring from the same source, yet all are different expressions of Me, and every stage of every wave is a being, an expression of I AM. Yet you think yourselves the only intelligence in the universe? In fact, you think yourselves the only intelligence on Earth. But Earth is intelligence itself, and each aspect of Her life, on its own wave, journeys forth. Each tree is an expression of Me and has being, sentience and intelligence as do thee. The substance of the rock is not the rock, indeed, as the matter of your body is not you, nor My substance wholly Me. Should a Martian, seeing your body, say, 'Ah, this is human, it expresses God, it has no intelligent life inside'?

All the material of the Earth is organised by intelligence foreign to thee, and in your ignorance and arrogance you treat as lifeless all the beings of Earth that are, like you, expressions of Me. Different waves of Me you may be, but you cannot escape that your fates, your lives, are intertwined with these. The Earth is made of a multitude of waves, their patterning following the design of My thought that shapes both the physical world and the evolution of all that unfolds *as* 'the world'.

All of My creation is an exercise in cooperation. As each part of God's apparent duality mirrors the other, so each part of a planet's evolvement depends, thrives or languishes upon the evolution of the other parts. The fire, earth, air and water of planet Earth do not assemble randomly into rocks, butterflies, trees and seas. No! Each of these materials is organised according to the evolving intelligence designed to build with these. Humans have called them by many names from elves and fairies to devils and demons, and monsters of the deeps. The subject of the waves of other being is so vast we can do naught but introduce it here.

Behind each element is being, just as behind each human there can be said to be one kind of intelligence, of being. These elements have sprung as we have seen, from the orderly unfoldment of God's being, unfoldment that ensures that the characteristics of a plane will be as God has 'imagined' it to be. Behind each element is a driving, raw, intelligent power—beings so great and vast, humans cannot yet imagine what this means. These high energies that come more directly from Me than anything you as human beings have seen, shaped the Earth in ages past but still they sit there, behind all Earthly 'things'. From their work they spawned a multitude of aspects of themselves, designed to carry out refinements in the making of the world. Are these no less than the great Solar angels which, splitting and dividing aspects of themselves gave rise to all of you? For it is humanity that a part of the Solar angels express. Sparkling waves of Light you may be, but beside you are a multitude of other sparkling waves of Light. Indeed!

Make no mistake that the great beings of the elements express My Will as surely as the most enlightened of thy souls express My Will through their service and alignment to Me. The creation and evolvement of the Earth is following My Plan and is just a part of a greater plan. Who are you, called 'man,' to interfere with My Plan? Truly, dominion is mastery, but it is mastery of the lesser aspects of oneself, and your lack of recognition of anything else that is Me, beside you in the Earth, is surely a lesser aspect of thee.

At every level of being this intelligence of nature surrounds you, and the Earth—if you could see it as the collection of patterned energies it is—is organised by a multitude of intelligent beings, who being more cognisant of you than you of them, willingly sacrifice their own comfort and peace of mind to carry out their tasks and serve, regardless of the cruelty and ignorance of mankind.

The Earth is a living being, made up of living beings. They are invisible to your human eye as the souls of one another are invisible to your eyes. But to see and cooperate with those beings has been part of your being. In the past it has been and is now also. To obtain a future bright with energy, it must also be. For energy is what life on this cosmic physical plane precisely means. You have thought it about manifestation, but manifestation is an effect, not a cause, of energy.

What you consider 'wild' on Earth is no accident, but the deliberate building of a perfect powerhouse of energy. 'Sacred' places, groups of trees, rocks, places in the mountains, and such things as these are not a fancy of primitive imagining, but the intelligence of Earth creating places of energetic generation.

The paths of evolution of the elemental beings are different from the evolutionary paths of you as human beings, it is true, but you are bound to each other as all aspects of Me are bound to Me. Therefore, you cannot escape, eventually, your sharing in each other's evolution. But do not project to the elemental world your human perceptions. They are different from you energetically and manifestly, and their manifesting will depend on that aspect of My nature they express. Some may seem monstrous and strange, foreign to you, and others, more in tune with the elemental makeup of your own bodily, emotional and mental history on Earth, will be more acceptable and compatible to you.

What I have called My elemental world, ranges in being from the raw (to you 'primitive') beings of the water, earth, fire, rocks, etc. to the more advanced conglomerates of beings who organise complex combinations of matter, combining all the elements of fire, earth, water, air. Their intelligence is behind every material composition, and in the bodies of plants, rocks, trees. And what of your body? You say it was God created thee but assume yourselves to be the only intelligent expression of God there is! How few amongst you can order thought *consciously* to materialise it as matter? Precious few masters amongst thee!

By your intelligence you manipulate that which has already been created to combine it in different ways, to 'create' something new. But this is not creation, just re-combination, or re-constitution. It is the great beings and their lesser beings who carry out Creation and each of them evolving as you are, back to their own God source.

Even the constitution of your body has an elemental being working in obedience and cooperation with you. You command it through your emotions until you consciously 'take command' and enlist its cooperation in obedience to the higher aspects, the mental, soul and spiritual you. Your world is truly then not one of independence and isolation but relationship and cooperation. At all levels, relationship effects you, bouncing you unwittingly against the boulders you have created, or steering with clear sight your boat of life through recognition and cooperation with all that consciousness has created that co-exists at every plane with you.

At every stage and way of being you have a chain of command available to you, from the elemental past and the 'lowest' physical manifestation of you, to the highest angelic being that you also are. You sit, humankind, in the middle, hovering around your heart, unsure whether your dwelling's in the bowels of the Earth's past or in the stars. The truth is that you are everywhere that you have been, in all paths and places, travelling on God's breath in each moment on every plane from star to Earth and back again. Can you ever live in a box again?

The Unfolding

The instant that divinity takes a breath, duality is created and 'separation' begins. For to breathe is to create two from One, an out from an in, and in that instant the in and the out breath rush to reunite with each other, for they are always bound to be the One which they are, and the rushing of their reuniting creates the third of the Trinity of Creation, and thus relationship is born.

The in-breath draws upon all that God is, the quiescence you call female from which the substance of Being is drawn. The out-breath propels, for it is the power of Will, causing the dividing. The substance, being of One, must attract back what belongs to itself as One, thus we call it Love. But these two, Love and Will are really One, and the child of their seeming division must propel from the Father (Will) back into the Mother through Love/attraction and the apparent Trinity is born. Apparent, because all takes place simultaneously for that which is undivided cannot in Truth be separated from itself.

The game of Creation is instantly and endlessly played, unfolding as Laws which mirror the Oneness which it both is and expresses. The Son, the third attribute of Truth, creates of itself another four. Thus your seven planes of the macrocosmic and the microcosmic are born. What you call Creation, we have named Unfolding, because it better serves at this time for your understanding that Creation is well described as the Unfolding of thought, and because that which you think is created never truly leaves its creator within which it resides. This is true whether the thoughts be of God itself or of you who are an extension of Him.

The 'physical' expression of the three attributes of divinity are: cosmic fire, through which divine Will finds expression in the cosmos; the void of God's night in which all potentiality lies and from which all 'things' wave forth in the great rays of Light; and pranic light which comes from the interplay of Will on substance, the Father and the Mother, the fires and the void. But they are One and their constant 'division' leads to constant 're-uniting,' thus the motion of Creation which we have described as a wave, is born. And the wave, while seemingly a wave of pranic light is also the Will and Stillness of God, thus in all stages of the wave the Trinity dwells, and each thing contains within it those three things, thus the Power, Love and Intelligence of the One God is made manifest.

God is infinite, thus the 'movement' of His unfolding creation can go on forever, but it is the nature of the physical plane universe that to manifest at any level, movement must be 'stopped' or bounded. Thus it is that the attribute of divinity we have called Relationship or Intelligence creates a boundary around its movement between Will and substance and this, at whatever level it occurs, we call 'form'. Form then, is bounded or frozen motion, and so it is that perception comes into being for perception is the direct result of the bounding or 'freezing' of the movement of the Trinity at a particular point.

Thus from the movement of Relationship is created a fourth aspect, boundary or concretisation, the 'freezing' of the flowing unfoldment of God's thinking. So the movement of God's thinking is 'solidified'. 'Four' then, can be said to be the creation of 'matter' and the fourth engenders from its own nature four that appear apart from the Trinity from which they came and in which they still in Truth reside.

The cosmic fire of divine Will is rendered or bound in form as the fire of matter as is embodied in the sun. The substance of the void is rendered or bound as water. So it is that fire is called masculine for it actively 'solidifies' the 'Father' attribute of God and water is said to be feminine for it manifests the 'Mother' attribute of God. From the relation of these two with each other, earth and air are born for this being the level of bounding there must be four or they would be not perceived as solidified. Thus the three become the seven and of the four much more will be said.

The unfoldment of Creation is constantly repeating its nature, for its attributes cannot be but what they are. So, the Trinity is in everything and manifestation at every stage is grouped in fours. The One unfolds as three and the three as four, then the four returns to the three and the three returns to One.

Such is the unfolding and folding of Creation—the movement of God's thinking breathing in and out. And always within this breathing the patterns of repetition hold. Creation is an unfoldment of that which is complete into what is seemingly incomplete. Each side of duality seeks its other half and this seeking we have called relationship. The unfolding is a 'journey' from and to completion and the laws by which the journey is bound are simply the nature of that which is unfolding. Thus are numbers born. Number, as we have said, describes these laws and the relationship of the four with each other and with its origin, the Trinity, gives rise to what you call proportion and harmony.

What we have here described is of the cosmic physical plane. But this is not the only possibility of unfoldment of divinity, and you need first to master your part in the unfoldment of your own plane before you concern yourself with the infinitude of the rest! Ah what a game here is played in the constant unfolding—of a flower, a sea, the kingdoms of the air, the rocks, Earth and thee.

Because God is perfection, the basic movement of our universe is round, and of the sphere we have spoken elsewhere. When fiery Will and cohering Love 'divide' the Oneness of God, a relationship of division (or 'two') is born. In this sense Will can be said to be the dividing force and Love to attract, creating a motion 'forward' and 'back;' 'forward,' away from each other and 'back' together. The relationship between the two creates, as we have seen, the third, and the third creates the fourth.

This in turn creates a relationship between the four and the three. This relationship creates the fifth impetus in the unfolding and it is this fifth which creates what you see as a movement forward. Thus the universe is said to move both spherically, (back) towards perfection, and forward, (through division.) But perfection is its original state or Truth and that which is moving away is attracted back, and the motion forward, being attracted back creates a spiral.

So it is that the universe of God moves at once spherically, forward and spirally. Behind all manifested creation is this unfolding movement—rounding, forward and back. So when the spiral, which you feel as 'time' seems to take you away from the divine, know that it cannot really be, for you *are* the divine, and the motion will spiral you back (in time) to the perfection you have always been.

Sound and light, as we have said before, are the two sides of a wave that propel its motion. Actually, it is clearer for your understanding now, to say that sound is the propelling force and light the resultant reflection. Thus we have duality—Will (sound) acting on Substance (intelligence) producing Love (light), the interaction creating movement—the wave.

Sound draws the shape of a thing out of the void. Thus to make the sound that something *is*, is to 'create' it. It is to name it, for the true sense of naming is to make the sound of the 'shape' that the thing is. Both sound and shape conform to, or rather express, laws of harmony and these harmonies are the *order* of Unfolding that *is* divine magic, for of it creation comes.

So, each shape is a sound, an energy called forth in particular assembly from the substance or void of God. Hence, as your scientists know, sound can create or destroy. Can you see then, why the mightiest of the mighty cannot be named except by itself, for to name it would be to sound it, to bring one's own sound into resonance with its sound, and its sound is too great a power for anything lesser than itself to wield. From this truth of sound has grown the magic of spells, a long forgotten art once wielded by the high, but now become the plaything of storytellers and would-be magicians of small, and usually selfish, intent.

Beware the sounds your children hear. Sound shapes their world as truly as it shapes the universe. Every energy has sound, and the discerning can discover in every energy, its sound. Everything in your universe can be heard. Every state of being is an energy, which is a sound-created shape. So think not only on what sound you hear, but on what sound all that is in your life creates. When the energies of your life—your language, art, building, music and so forth—are drawn from the Laws of Harmony, grace, balance and proportion unfold themselves, and the shapes of your world sing as the pyramids sing, as the flower sings, as the water in a storm or in a tinkling fall, sing.

The body and soul expressing divine Light sings that Light and thus those bodies are shaped by the sound of its wave. The density and shape of matter has its sound, and therefore its inherent energy. A great stone rightly shaped has very different sound (and energy) from a rude wooden hut but fashioned carelessly.

Mathematics, sound, light, harmony—all are Truth or manifestations of Truth once you discover their unfoldment from divinity rather than trying to make up your own laws of mathematics, sound etc. which are just a parody of divinity, rewarding perhaps to the intellect and personality, but of little use to the greater depths that the seeker seeks to know.

As all sound comes from the One sound, and all Light from the One Light, so the One contains all the Sound and all the Light that it is. Be it a structure, a piece of art, a dance or a song, if it is according to divine intent and unfolding, it too will contain all that the One contains. A true symbol therefore is one in which all Truth can be found. It offers an infinitude of revelation and is therefore bound not by the time and place of its 'creating,' for its creation lies not in the whim of a human personality but in the source of One—God itself or Truth, as we have named it. Most of the symbols of your world then, are signs not symbols, for they display association not Truth. Their association is with man-ufactured idea, not a manifestation of Truth.

It is only possible for myth to embody Truth when the mythmakers really understand the Truth that the making of the myth symbolises, as it is their expression of the Truth, derived from purity of intent—intent aligned with divine Will. That others may not understand the Truth or have revelation of the Truth behind the myth does not alter the wisdom acquired by its creators, nor rob the myth of the original energy of its maker's intent. The Truths of the myth remain for the pure of intent to discover again. The ability to manifest Truth is wisdom indeed, but not all mankind is, as yet, capable of being wise in their consciousness on the Earth plane.

The sides of the triangle extend, as we have said, beyond their points of intersection. The triangle perpetually repeats itself, for is it not the Trinity? It is no accident that man is the fourth kingdom. As we have seen the Trinity gives rise to or 'creates' the fourth, thus manifesting itself in matter. Man then, as he now stands, sits between two trinities—the natural triad of mineral, vegetable and animal 'beneath' him, and the three kingdoms of soul, spirit and divinity above him. Man is the solidification of both, at the base of a triangle, which sits above him and at the top of a triangle, which sits below him. (In shape this can be represented two ways, as a diamond or an X.) It is the task of man, the middle kingdom, to raise those in the triangle below to the heights, and to bring the heights of the planes above him into the lower. However it is described, it is again a case of duality being pulled back into Oneness again.

Now, as the triangle perpetuates itself, it is mirrored in all that is created from it, although its manifestation is a continual process of balance (as it returns to its Oneness) and imbalance (as it strives to divide or to express division). Some see this as struggle, but that is a perception of the stage of man as the fourth kingdom, the stage of concretisation, the square. But as man moves from an embodiment of this square back to the divine Trinity through the planes currently above him, his perception will be one of harmonious movement, not warring imbalance.

The true grace of this movement is manifested in what you have named the golden mean, or section, and gold it is indeed, for golden is the colour of the alchemist's prize, the master who is not a victim of the apparent whims of the world but who lives in the Light of understanding, his experience transformed. He wields the power of the word in line with his Creator's intent. What greater gold can you seek than this? Truly, the alchemist is above mortality for his body is filled with Light and his succour comes not from the kingdoms below him but from those above and thus he feeds literally, on Light.

The Trinity contains all, and from it all your realities are born. The three attributes of the Trinity—Will, Love and Intelligence—are represented by the triangle. The three sides of the triangle are in relationship to each other. It is this relationship that creates the space between them, the centre of the triangle that is the fourth arising from the relationship of the three. This *is* space, born as and of the fourth, and the triangle is multiplied by that space to give physicality because for the triangle to have physicality it must be repeated four times, creating the tetrahedron. This is what you call a three-dimensional figure, though it would be better described as the fourth dimension, in which the fourth reflects, in never-ending perpetuation, the triangle to itself. From the fourth then is the three reflected and the seven planes of cosmic physicality are born.

Yet it is not the tetrahedron but the pyramid that is chosen as embodiment of the truths of the cosmic physical plane. The sides of the pyramid demonstrate the Trinity and its base the square, the concretisation of the Trinity as matter and space, just as the space inside the triangle and the tetrahedron show that the relationship of the attributes of the Trinity to each other create the boundary of space.

The triangle of the pyramid's sides and the square at its base give the seven great waves or rays of the cosmic physical plane, and the shape of the pyramid, when correctly drawn in right proportion, also embodies the measurements of the circle which can be scribed around it, as the symbol of Creation rightly both gives rise to and embodies it. Thus the pyramid tracks the solar system from where it has come to where it is and where it will be. For in the first round, the creation of matter, the matter was infused with intelligence as it needs be. For matter arose from the fourth aspect in the relationship or intelligence of the Trinity, thus it is only right sequentially that matter be first infused with intelligence.

But as we have seen, all returns to the Oneness of God and in the returning, matter must also be infused or 'raised' by its infusion with the other aspects of the Trinity, thus now, in this round, matter is being infused with Love and the wisdom of Spirit. This applies to the human kingdom as well. Thus this round of the solar system strives toward the Trinity as it moves back towards the divine state of Oneness through Love.

We have said that perfection, or the divine state, is spherical, in graphic representation, and it is indeed sphericity towards which the solar system inevitably travels. The spherical round of the solar system is eons away and this need not concern you except in so far as to understand that this macrocosmic movement or plan, is repeated at every level of being.

Thus the sphere embodies or symbolises the return to the undivided Oneness and in that returning matter will be infused with the Will of divinity until the returning is complete, and what lay in the void as the potentiality of these worlds will have been explored. Yet whether that potentiality will have been exhausted in every possibility, is not for us to say. See then, how, as we have said, all things are raised and returned to their source of consciousness again?

Time & Space

There is much more needs be said of number, but what has been said will for here, suffice. When you look into the triangle you peer into a space, and indeed, it is the relationship of the attributes of the Trinity from which arises—out of the third aspect, activity or Intelligence—space, or more correctly put, the illusion or perception of space. For space is but one view and the 'laws' of space do not hold when you change your view. Space is an aspect of the cosmic physical plane. Move out of the layer or plane which manifests space, and it disappears, for it is, as we have just said, a perception rather than a truth.

In this respect, all four aspects of Creation that arise as materiality from the third attribute of divinity, which we have named Intelligence, can be said to be illusory, for they are products of the apparent movement of the One created by the *appearance* of the Trinity. Whereas the Trinity describes the inherent attributes of the One Truth, that which naturally manifests is the playing out of possibilities arising from the relationship between those attributes.

Space is 'created' only within a particular band of the waveform spawned by the movement of the unfolding of God's thought as 'creation'. It is, if you like, a range of frequencies.

Time, as we have said, is 'created' by the apparent distance of a waveform from its still point at the source. Time again is an illusion, for the source (God) does not move, but only *is*. From where you stand however, the thoughts or unfolding of God seem to move and as a wave of God's thought 'travels' back and forth creating its expression, it seems from your perception to alter. It is the unfolding of its potential, the manifestation of all that it is, that creates the illusion of change, and therefore of time. Time can only be described in terms of movement, from one point to another, or one state to another. That which is truly still does not change and is therefore not subject to, or part of, time.

The true master, therefore, while dealing in the realms concerned with time, is unaltered and unmoved himself by time, having centred his consciousness permanently on the still source of his being from which his God force issues forth.

Time, as you know it, marks arbitrary points of your choosing, in your perception of change. Because the unfolding of God's thinking flows out in patterns of proportion and harmony it is natural that your measuring of 'events' reflect these harmonies of unfoldment. This should be true of all your measures since they represent to you those harmonies made concrete, as they echo at the level of the physical plane.

In your perception then, time is both vertical and horizontal. Vertical, because it traces what you see as the movement of God's thinking, unfolding as the planes of Creation; consciousness unfolding into manifestation at all levels. Horizontal, because you can measure it as consistent within your own plane of material consciousness. But time is also simultaneous or holographic because God is not in Truth divided, and all that seems to be manifest sequentially is still contained as the One and is therefore all in existence simultaneously. This is why you are multidimensional beings, and why you can, when you master the 'why' and the 'how,' access any plane or aspect of that One consciousness that God is, and of which you are an expression.

While the first two views of time are linear, the third is not, and this gives rise to the discrepancy often felt by you, that what you desire that requires assistance of your higher Selves does not always manifest 'quickly'. To those in the consciousness of the higher planes the perception of time is necessarily non-linear, and what there is simultaneous, to you may not be so. It is your perception of time that increases your perception of separation from Me, from each other, and from the other aspects and dimensions of yourselves that do not function in the same linear time zone as that in which you perceive yourself to be.

It is not so difficult, were you to practice it but a little, to experience the consciousness of Life as simultaneous and thus free yourselves of the restrictive thinking and experience of your linear and vertical time zones. These are not wrong views of time, but they are limited and not a completion of the Trinity as expressed through 'time,' since they leave out the third or principle unifying attribute, which enables sense to be made of the other two, and right perspective to be gained of your part in the unfolding of the divine Plan.

Space is the fourth aspect and arises from the relationship of the attributes of the Trinity to each other. It is a plane or section of a vast and complex group of waveforms at the furthest point from their still point at their source. It is at the same time both a shape and the complementarity of the shape of an idea that sits as potential in the void. A shape or idea does not crystallise into form until it is bounded by its complementary shape. Thus the physical plane appears to be a plane of limitation and indeed in the sense that it is a plane created by boundaries, it is indeed limited. But it is bounded only by the limits set by the nature of the idea that sent it forth.

Thus it is the square or the fourth that arises from the Trinity. It is dual in nature, expressing at once an idea and its complementarity. (As does the key and the impression it makes in the 'clay' of universal substance.) Its duality can be said to be the relationship of the Trinity reflecting itself; the son reflecting back to its parents their duality; Intelligence by its very existence reflecting back to Love and Will their apparent division as separate attributes of the Oneness that they are. Hence the square of matter is two triangles mirroring each other and thus the pyramid embodies both the Trinity (the triangle of its sides) and materialisation, (the square of its base and the four triangles of its top) the life of the Trinity *as* the material or physical plane.

In physical plane reality the four sides of the square which actually 'create' physicality by bounding an idea and thus creating form, are manifested also as the four elements. It is from the interplay of these waveforms that the structure of the physical world is born. This is, of course, a simplification but it suffices now, for you need first grasp an understanding of the order behind God's unfolding to enable your own unfolding of understanding.

What, in summary then, it is important at this point to understand, through this reading and through contemplation of your own, is that the One appears to divide, in the expressing of its thought, and from the relationship of this division of two, the Trinity arises. And from the three the fourth and the four are born, and thus the cosmic physical plane comes to be, in which the One has become the seven and so the seven planes, layers or 'heavens' in which you play, are the layers of this 'reality'.

Because time mirrors the attributes of the universe (as all attributes of the One must mirror and contain each other), time is holographic (spherical), linear and spiral. Each of these attributes of time can serve you, and your use of time need not be confined to its linear attribute.

Time is a manifestation of the movement of the universe and in this sense is illusory since God moves not. Yet it unfolds according to the Laws of Unfoldment. In its holographic nature, time can be used to heal outside of what you normally see as the constraints of time. Since in the hologram or sphere of time, all things exist simultaneously, a healing at one point in the hologram affects other parts of the hologram. Thus, when in one lifetime you heal aspects of yourself that have been out of harmony, balance and grace, you are simultaneously affecting those aspects of yourself in other lifetimes. This is also why karma is wiped from the souls of the enlightened for by their change of consciousness they change all aspects of themselves on other time zones. Do you see then, how you are said to be multidimensional? Ponder on this holographic nature of time and you will realise why attending vigilantly to the quality of your thinking/feeling/consciousness in every moment in continuous acknowledgement and participation of now, is vital to your well being.

In the spiral attribute of its nature, time allows you to re-visit, but at a higher 'level' the cyclical events of the flowing out of God's thought. Thus you 'progress' by attending to the forward nature of the spiralling, rather than to moving backwards down the spiral.

The linear aspect of time allows you to deal step by step with one aspect of life. How limited and false then is your thinking that this step by step view is the only reality in which you exist! These three attributes of time function simultaneously. It is, as always, a matter of which you will attend to. The illusion lies in thinking that time has only one reality, forward or back.

As consciousness moves to higher vibrations, closer to the source or Stillness of God, so the 'movement' of time seems to speed up. Actually, you are moving towards sphericity, and therefore you are more conscious of the holographic or simultaneous nature of time, hence 'events' seem to rush into each other. As the consciousness of Earth itself rises, so will this effect of time speeding up be increased. For you and your state of consciousness and that of the Earth are part of a planetary and solar dance in which all create and experience the movement and music of the cosmic physical plane.

A little thought will show you the relationship of time to space. They are, as colour and sound are the two sides of

Light, two sides of manifestation that are a bound 'duality' that is in fact One. Once you can remove your mind from its fixed point to acceptance of these seeming paradoxes, a whole new understanding will open before you and it becomes a universe not of confinement but of infinite and joyous play.

The Planes

As the great waveforms of God's thought unfold, at each
stage of unfoldment, a sea of vibrations resounds, and thus
the planes are 'formed'. So great is the thinking of God, that
it defies the tiny mind of man to understand, but as you
return your consciousness from this tiny focus as humankind
to the expanded consciousness of the Oneness whence you
came, you do indeed, step by step, begin to comprehend.
But for your understanding to progress, and your picture to
widen, your former view must be rendered up and discarded
for the greater view, as a growing child must discard his tiny
clothes for bigger ones when his body grows.

So, abandon now your view of the world as the complete
and only view, and stop to contemplate myriad worlds that
be in planes of different view. For now, let your understanding be this; that the waveforms of God's thinking form
planes of seemingly greater and greater complexity and
density as they move further from their source. But they
all remain in the One, and thus it is that only in seeming
do some aspects of Creation become separated from the
rest, flying off as if independent from the thought which
sent them forth.

As each great wave sounds forth, colour, light and sound
are the product, or rather the intrinsic character of its vibration, and as the note of the bell subtly alters as it lessens in
strength and intensity from its sounding to its being spent,

so the great wave of God's thinking will seem different at its source from its extension at its 'ending'. Yet it is all the same note, all the same wave. Thus in consciousness you can travel 'back' along your wave, and experience the resonance at each of the planes created by the vibration of the wave. The closer you get to your source in God, the purer the colour and the purer the light and sound of the plane. The closer to your source in God you go, the greater must be your power.

So it is that the learned rightly describe a multitude of planes and also rightly teach that in your own realm in the journey, (so far as it can be seen and comprehended at this point) the journey of you as a being of your solar system and its world, lies in a seven-fold plane and inside these, the many sub-planes. And this is, as it should be, all that God encompasses to you, yet God is more than this. Inexpressible is the might and power that lies beyond this view of God, greater even than the highest planes that can be taught or glimpsed in miniscule appreciation by you. So, be assured, that you can never fall from the net of God, for the cosmic fire that will burn in the end the final shell of dross from even the most enlightened beings at the source of your realm, will carry all to ever greater realms.

As the great waves of God's thinking ripple through His substance, so that substance is 'electrically' changed and formed and re-formed, and the idea of Creation dances in the mind of God. Not all the waves of God's thinking wander to the farthest reaches of density as you have done. Some remain close to their source, and they seem to you great explosions of light forming planes of pure colour and sound that are themselves a universe of knowing and creative beings of immeasurable magnitude and power.

Others retain raiment of pure Light but extend further, dancing on the edges of your world of echoes. These you count among the angels who appear to you in heavenly form, their wings a measure of their might and lightness and their freedom from the weights that tie mankind to his round of life, death and rebirth. Their warmth and Light resonates with the heart of every human being that opens to welcome them, to every human mind that aspires to their heights, and every human who feels his spirit fly beside them. They are the beings who carry the messages of God in song—tantalising sound that beckons the wandering pieces of Him home.

They hold the purity of their being within the reach of any who look up within themselves to read the glory written there. Knowing them gives you knowledge for they join you to the planes of knowing where Truth is held in colour, sound and Light in a formless sea. Enough form the angels have themselves to show you places that seem formed to you, that most amongst you think is heaven, yet it is but a stage, a plane amongst many heavenly planes.

Each plane is a level of understanding. While the planes, and the levels of consciousness required for awareness of them, can be described as hierarchical, nevertheless, because each level is a stage in the extension from the source, (which we call 'God') they are One. The 'paradoxes' of Truth must be grasped through contemplation, for words merely confirm what you already understand, or serve to trigger a pattern of thought that leads to your understanding. It is the duality of words that creates the seeming paradoxes. When grasped, it is seen that Truth contains no paradoxes, it just is, and we describe that nature of Truth or isness as 'One,' for it is undivided.

Everything that extends from God is already complete before its extension into manifestation. As God is all there is, God itself is complete and so must be all that rests in God or appears to move as creations of or within God. The immediate source of your being then, is one of the great waves emanating from the Silence and Stillness of God, shining forth as Light from His void, whence all substance is. Each solar system then, is a pattern of waves emanating from a greater wave. These waves are formed by the harmonies of cosmic Law, and it is of these harmonies that what man sees as number, is born.

As you return in consciousness towards the source of your wave, the lightness, the illumination of your being increases, because what you attend to you manifest. How can you not when consciousness is the cause of effects? Any point along the wave can be described as manifestation. It is just that the manifestation varies in density at every part of the extension of the wave.

This is why you are the angel from which you have come, and the higher you rise on the wave of your being, the more you are joined with the other 'parts' that also extend from that source, their own solar wave. We seem to have reduced the process of creation, of manifestation, to a scientific description of 'electric light waves,' but this is a misleading description for each level of this Light wave is a state of being and this being can rightly, from your own vantage point, be seen as made up of celestial beings who do indeed have reality as great and powerful beings with countenance and abilities that seem to those at your point along the wave, magical.

Let the ease of their being inspire you to know that you are also capable of being as they are. Yes. Each of you is surrounded by angels for the higher vibrations of your wave 'surround' you. It requires only the lifting of your mind to the vibration that they are, for them to communicate with you and for you to learn to be as they are.

It is the 'movement' of the manifestation of consciousness back up a wave, towards its source, that you have interpreted as 'evolution'. A more accurate term would be 'return'. Thus your world is on a journey of return. All the kingdoms of your world—mineral, vegetable, animal, human—are on this 'journey' of return, seemingly split off on the 'separate' waves of their own manifestation. In this sense each has its own evolutionary path, but in the end, all the separate waves of your world rejoin the greater wave from which they sprang forth. Thus it can also be said that they are on the same journey back to the source. This separateness is only a seeming for all remains One—diamond, rock, tree, flower, bee, elephant and thee—in the uncreated Stillness of God. As you journey back in consciousness to your source, so these kingdoms journey with you, and as the journey proceeds, forms are discarded or changed, as they must be when consciousness does not remain the same.

Allow that all are rising with you, and know that as your form must eventually be totally infused with Spirit, so must they, and to this end, through your own Love and enlightenment, much assistance can be given to them. This recognition gives rise to respect and co-operation, whereas exploitation delays the happiness of all.

All of the kingdoms here named have likewise their angel forms, the higher planes of consciousness from which those kingdoms spring. These devas or angelic beings are indeed the architects of their lesser forms as your angelic being is the architect of your form. But do not blame your angelic Self for the faults of your form! Remember that each level of consciousness creates or manifests its own form.

Can you see then, that the joining of your higher intent with the devic intent can produce in your realm an Earth of exquisite beauty, built not on strife but on joy and delight in the sharing of Life? It is possible indeed for the lion to lie down with the lamb, and the speed or delay of this day lies in your hands. On which of the many planes will you play today?

Identification

Your thoughts are like conduits of electricity. They allow
energy to follow in a particular direction. Every doubt, every
fear, sends the energy of your life flowing in the direction
determined by that quality. The quality of that choice must
come back to you, sooner or later, unless you find the power
to negate and redirect that energy you have sent forth. The
assistance you receive from your soul and those who assist
you from the higher planes can increase immeasurably when
you remain, regardless of circumstance, in a state of calm,
aware more of the peace, tranquillity and joy of heaven
than of the upheavals of your world.

Do not always presume that such help will be of a physical nature. To the higher realms the physical is hardly real
and it is not specific situations to which these higher planes
respond but to a quality of energy. If a child falls and cuts
its knee, how much easier is administration of your nursing
and sympathy if the patient remains calm and receptive,
and how much quicker can the remedy be found. And so
it is with the problems you experience as part of being in
your world.

Those of great countenance shine forth, regardless of
man's ability or willingness to receive the benefit of their
being. Access to the upliftment and assistance of those
higher realms is like a shop where payment is made by your
practised skill in the ability to calmly reflect what you wish

to receive. And how much assistance can you render in the world by your ability to be a recipient of such bounty! Unless they are physically present on Earth those in higher realms must work through the good agency of those who understand. How else can they have a conduit from Heaven to the world of man?

Honesty, lack of interest in glamour and a constant focus on that which is of noblest and highest good is its own protection. Right focus of your intent ensures the harmlessness of the help you request. Remember always, although the outcome may be precise and not always what you expect, you should not try to dictate to God the best solution for your dilemmas. Would you tell the devas how to design a leaf, or the mountains where and how to sit upon the Earth? Nay, and neither should you dictate to those who see the higher way and greater view exactly what it is that they should do and how their help should come to you.

Go forth to them with humble heart that is filled with Love and joy that they should care a jot for you. Despite your former ignorance of them, they welcome you, expending energy and Love to lift and make the pathway easier to see for you. Do not blame them when the way seems strewn with boulders. Are not some mountains harder to climb than others? Cease to measure in human terms. You do not measure a journey by sea by how much water there was in the ocean or how high the waves became, but rather by your handling of the conditions and your success in bringing your boat to the other shore. Learn to live on the other shore, even though you seem to dwell in the physical ocean of storms.

Are not the greatest leaders the ones who can respond to circumstance as the circumstance might need, but who keep about them level headed calm and think not of themselves but of the overall good of those in their charge? All of you who are to some degree spiritually awake, have such responsibilities as these. What bankruptcy of spirit has a doctor who will not administer to a patient in need? God refuses no one. How can that which simply *is*, sometimes be not there? God does not dispense gifts only to the good, but simply returns like for like as elsewhere in these books has been said.

Such a challenge is the elimination of fear! When all about you crumbles and you feel as if the very mountain tries to pull you down, remember to take another view, stop and see the quality of energy that comes from you. What quality is that cauldron that whirls inside of you? The boulders you place in your path are emotions—emotions of the lower self. You may label them as pride, conceit, insecurity, carelessness, false humility or any number of other labels. All in the end are a non-acceptance of the divinity of who and what you really are. To screen all 'others' out of your thinking and be aware only of the divine in you eliminates the falsity of all the emotions that stand between you and 'God within'. Examine every motive of your utterances. Examine every thing you have blamed for your circumstances and you will find you have created circumstances by the writing you have placed upon the page you call your 'life'.

Every self-deception brings not that which the personality desired but whatever quality of life that deception in its essence was. Whatever problem you think you have in your life—money, health, loneliness—are not thrust upon you by an angry God, but wrought deep within the consciousness you are. Blame yourself not for these falsities and lacks, for such a blame is itself a lie, a false humility, inverted pride.

Let the spirit child in you take charge. Abandon social games and take the many hands that God as Spirit offers you. Start giving to others the joy of your soul. This giving takes no effort, and requires not the 'riches' of your world, and yet it is a gift more uplifting than all the money millionaires have made, for is it not the *presence* of Christ that heals and 'saves?' Are you created outside of God? Of course not! How could you be since God is in truth the totality, the essence, the onlyness of all there is?

Within, within! Always be centered on the divinity you are within. From that state right action flows, and all the things that you created, the misery of rampant personality, dissolve, if you are willing to let them go. But give in to the personality again, its need to control, and lo, back will those boulders be and back the limits and confines of that personality. Have the trust of God's child, but not carelessly, for carelessness is not a trait of divinity!

Fear is the teacher of men because it shows what is not, and teaches the mis-identifying soul what it is. We have talked of healing through identification with that which is higher. Fear is the reverse—it occurs when you identify with the lower distortion. In the cosmic physical universe, driven by mind and manifesting through mind impressing itself on universal Substance, how could it not be that what you identify with, you are? For that is where your attention is, that is the shape of your impression on universal Substance. This is true both for the simple and the apparently complex. Your soul is a state and stage of being. It resides on a certain plane *because* its resonance, its constitution, or vibratory being, is such that it *is of* that plane.

But your soul is an extension of your higher Self or divine Being, and beyond that it is an extension of higher states of divinity which all but the most high are incapable of intuition or comprehension. These higher states are indeed planes beyond imagining. So let us content ourselves with but a little understanding of the lower planes that we call the cosmic physical universe that you might more quickly leave them behind and so take your substance and the other parts of God with you.

Remember that even the plane of the soul is physical—it still resides within that band of sub-planes which constitutes the cosmic physical plane, though we refer to what is higher as non-physical, because mankind cannot as yet see or function consciously on those higher planes. Yet in a sense he does, for as we have said, his soul resides there, and beyond is his higher Self. But the personality of man has forgot and what is forgotten is no longer a reality to the disconnected personality-mind.

How can this be, that the glory of the soul forgets itself in the mires of concrete form? This journey of soul is an exploration by God of Its potentially. Nothing happens that is not God exploring itself, plumbing the infinity of ways to be. You, as a soul, are an aspect of God exploring the potential of your own peculiar wave of being.

Whatever level you identify with determines the narrowness or breadth of your thought and the experience of your life. Do not confuse this with focus. To be focused is to gather one's energies through discrimination of the mind and direct them as one stream to a particular goal. Focus produces more potent action, gathering in, not scattering, energy.

Identification comes before focus. What kind of energy do you identify with? That determines the quality and direction of your focus and determines the kind of results. A fanatic is focused, but he identifies with a narrow idea, or the distortion of a great and inspired idea into a small selfish one, even though he may think it noble and a source of pride!

The wisdom-giver, the person who steers mankind to that which is higher, identifies with the broader principles of universality, but in focusing his energies to a particular task, does not lose sight of these broader principles. His identification remains with the higher, unselfish intent.

If those who have become expert at focusing their energies would change their identification from the narrow and divisive, and therefore inherently selfish, to the broader principles of unity, compassion and brotherhood, (in the spiritual sense) how quickly would humanity progress from suffering to a glorious expression of Life.

Contemplate for a while, the principles of unselfish concerns such as non-separateness, compassion, the upliftment of the whole for the good of the one, and the upliftment of the one for the good of the whole. Imagine how one's actions would alter if the heart-mind remains identified with these soul-plane characteristics and concerns. With what do you identify?

What does fear identify with? Always with loss of some kind, a physical loss (or damage), or an emotional loss. They are losses of an illusory nature for as you have begun to see, when consciousness is seated in the higher planes, that which is lower is seen as an illusion. An illusion is not real, therefore you are fearing to lose that which is not real, but you can only know the falsity of fear when you identify with that which is higher than what you fear to lose.

Fear comes from not seeing the larger picture. It is an error in which the mind identifies with a narrow, confined perception. It therefore binds and constrains you within a perceptual box.

Even a content personality can be confined within a box! Contentment arises when one's experience matches what one has chosen to identify as happiness-bringing. Thus, the person who places his identification purely in the physical will be content when his physical conditions match his ideal. He has contentment of a physical kind, but eventually, in the inevitable movement of the universe, his contentment will be shattered, either by a change of circumstances or by the pull of his own soul to fulfil its task; to raise matter to a higher note of being.

Then the yearning of the seeker after Truth will begin and the veil of illusion begin to break before his eyes. But before his soul can accomplish its purpose, the storms and earthquakes of change must rent his life. For how can a new form of being find a space before the old forms of thought are dissembled to clear that space for the new to be? After all, what is a state of being except an identification of consciousness with a pattern, an energetic configuration within a plane, a particular organisation of universal substance.

What we have called here, 'mind' could as easily be called 'Will'. When Will or mind identifies with a level of being it is simply directing its attention (force) onto universal substance, impacting and arranging that substance in accordance with the identification. The intelligence of Will is in its ability to discriminate as to the nature of the force or energy it exerts. The intelligence of substance lies in its ability to respond perfectly to the force of Will. These two, are after all, the two appearances we call duality which are in Truth the One thing, that we call God, and so we come back again to seeing that God cannot in Truth be divided. If this is the nature of God then obviously our striving must always be towards that Truth, and thus we know that to the extent that our thought and actions are not reflecting the ultimate unity of God, they are false.

Yet the personality lays many traps to veil from us what in actuality leads to Truth and what leads away. To advance, man must learn to recognise the pitfalls of the personality and recognise within himself what is a desire of the personality and what is a higher, seemingly often sacrificial desire of the soul. Only through the development of discrimination can one realise what it is that one is identifying with in any given situation or in any impulse to 'do' or to 'be'.

Identification with your soul rather than your personality, both requires detachment and brings detachment. This is because, by comparison, the higher plane is more 'detached' from the lower plane because the lower the plane, the more the consciousness is identifying with the form. This must be, because the lower the plane, the more 'formed' the wave-lengths of that plane are. Better put, physical form is created by the wavelengths of the lower plane. The wavelengths of the higher plane produce form that is less dense. This holds for all forty-nine sub-planes of the cosmic physical plane.

Identification is the nature of the journey into matter, but to raise matter, to infuse it with the consciousness of the higher planes, the soul (which is temporarily embodying itself in dense matter) must learn to be conscious of itself, not just as a personality (that part of itself which is projected into matter) but *at the same time* as a soul which is embodied at a higher plane. Can you see then, how even the attachments to the body of the soul will eventually have to be given up by the divine Life that you are for the awareness of the higher Self. So, as we have said, 'this journey never ends' at least, not to our seeming at this point.

As a personality, you identify with the external and the temporal, be it your culture, your appearance, your 'place' in society, your job, your family, your abode, your status, the things you own, the freedom you see yourself having or not having, and of course your religion, politics and opinions or lack thereof.

Ask yourself then, if any of these things with which you identify have reality in the plane of the soul. When you truly experience the plane of the soul, you shall smile tolerantly at this question. As your soul gains control of your life, the separative concerns of the personality give way to the broader concerns of the soul. The divisions so beloved of man give way to the inclusiveness of the soul wherein judgement of your fellow man is replaced by acceptance of his stage of journeying and error recognised with detachment and compassion, and without the fears, glamours and anguishes of the personality.

It is so Light, this plane of the soul, so content with being and yet secure with a solidity of reality that cannot exist in any temporal structures of Earth be it mountain or creed, dwelling place or philosophy. Of course, the soul must 'work' with the substance of Earth if it would raise that substance to consciousness of the higher planes, but it can only raise matter as high as its own identification allows during the course of its embodiment in matter. If the substance you use for your body (and the outer appearances of your life) is an instrument of the personality, not of the soul, how can it become infused with the vibration of the soul and thereby be raised in its consciousness to the plane of the soul?

Did we not tell you that with the devas you have co-created the world? Did we not also say that the elementals play the tunes that the devas sing? It is the elementals, the intelligences of form itself whom you raise when you allow your life and its expression (through form) to be infused by your soul.

The personality is not a sin, but a stage in the process of infusing matter with the Light of Self-awareness. The bringing of the personality to fruition through the raising of consciousness from the physical to the emotional to the mental planes, is the goal of every human being, for that in itself constitutes a glorious raising of matter. But once achieved, this achievement must be supplanted by the higher goal of raising consciousness to the plane of the soul and then beyond in the endless journey back on the inbreath of God to complete knowing of itself in its infinitude of possibility.

So, in the raising of your consciousness, in the supplanting of the life of personality with the life of the soul, the elementals must necessarily reorganise the matter under the command of your thought. As your thought is raised so are they, and as we have said before, you bring the lower kingdoms with you as you journey, for consciousness is One and all the kingdoms rise with you to the Light of the One Life that you and all that appears to be distinct from you, are.

Relationship

You cannot have physicality without the fourth. The tetrahedron demonstrates this for the square 'equals' solidification. The relationship of the attributes of God to each other unfold as shape. It is their shape *esoterically speaking*, that creates their reality. True mathematics is the discovery and description of these unfolding shapes, the properties of which govern reality.

It is these relationships which govern the shape of the waveform. It is these relationships modern man has unconsciously tried to represent in his architecture without understanding what drives him to do so, and with no comprehension of underlying principles of cosmic and therefore Earthly significance. It is only the fourth that need concern you at present, for it is that which holds time and is currently valid for your plane and experience of that plane. God's thinking spawns other relationships that you are not capable of comprehending at present. The analogy is that of base number systems—the rules hold true only for that base.

When the waveform hits a certain point in its unfolding, then the laws of the physical universe click into play. Because you are at the place along the waveform where the Trinity is the experience of the unity, it gives rise to certain relationships and the wave is 'bent' into the shapes determined by the relationship of the Oneness, experienced as the Trinity. An analogy for purposes of understanding, is that when the billiard ball hits the side of the table on a particular angle, it is that angle which governs what angle (direction) at which the ball will come *off* the side, and the force with which it hits will determine the speed. Esoterically, when applied to the planes; the speed is governed by Will, the angle by the relationship between the attributes of God in their unfolding as 'thinking'. It is the quality of the energy or thinking that determines the range of shapes in a plane. To this extent the plane is 'limited' to that quality.

To give you another description; the Light is 'bent' according to the shape of the thinking that sent it forth. This holds true at the human thinking level and at the level of God's thinking, since the human is just part of a chain of waveforms of God's thinking. It is your apparent ability for independent thought that causes you to think yourselves outside the rules of God's thinking and separate from Him. Fatalism is a distortion of the Truth that a shape of God's thinking cannot be anything other than what it is at that particular point in its unfoldment.

Because of the multi-dimensional nature of time, you can stay in one frozen moment, traverse the dimensions of time as a journey, or go around in loops of repetition, repeating the same 'shapes'. The fourth dimension, or what you call three-dimensional reality, is created by the relationship of the triangle with itself, whereupon its wave is reflected back as it hits the angle of its joining, creating the square, or fourth aspect. In this universe, the energy generated by the relationship of the three attributes of the Trinity to each other 'bounces' off the Trinity at what can be described as an 'angle of 90 degrees,' what you call a 'right angle'.

Although this happens within the Trinitiy, it creates a seemingly disparate shape which does not have the same angles as the triangle itself. It is only obtainable by dividing the triangle by a 'line' from its apex to the opposite side, (the base) splitting the triangle into a duality. While this creates a 'distortion' of the triangle's nature, it nevertheless reveals an internal potential, a potential already contained or inherent within the triangle.

The fourth dimension or 'square' that is created out of the Trinity is therefore, by its nature apparently divisive or fractionating. It is a stage in the movement of Creation 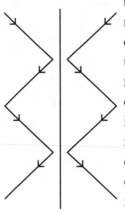 that spawns another series of creative movements, (5, 6 and 7) each with their own characteristics, but with a spiralling tendency back towards the Trinity itself, four being the midway point, the point of departure, but also of returning since it spawns another Trinity that returns, now with additional knowledge and experience of itself. ('Itself' being the original Trinity.) This 'descent' into matter is the Trinity's exploring of itself *in this particular direction* only.

If there are other possibilities within the Trinity, it is not for speculation here, except to say that from such other possibilities would a different universe of experience spring. Human mathematics, particularly 'sacred' geometry, is the attempt to describe or concretise these explorations of potential carried out by and within the Trinity. Because of the apparently 'fracturing' nature of the fourth as the triangle is divided to produce it, so the sense of separation is engendered by the consciousness exploring that possibility of densification into matter *in this way*, creating this particular 'universe' of a set of planes we call 'physical'.

As we have said, this in turn creates further relationships and expands the range of shapes, and therefore manifestation of the physical plane, but these other shapes are not our concern here. All we wish to do is to give you an understanding that in each plane, mechanisms are at play producing the experience and manifestation of that plane, and to broaden your realisation of the realties of Life available for any sentient being to experience.

They who understand are no longer imprisoned or confined in their experience by their lack of understanding. Make not of your minds a prison, but fill them with the Light of understanding. The greater your view, the greater will be your wisdom in the handling of that which is still imprisoned in the tiny view.

The fractured view is characteristic of and intrinsic to that which is fourth dimensional because such is the nature of that dimension. As we have said, it is created when the energy of the Trinity 'hits' the Trinity itself and is deflected at 'ninety degrees,' creating a certain level of materiality which you know as physical reality. Until your thinking returns to the Trinity and the unity inherent in the Trinity, it will always be fractured and separate, and has been poetically called the 'fall' or 'descent' into matter. It is only a fall when it is forgotten that it is simply one shape in an infinite possibility of shapes—one view in the infinity of God's view.

As the squareness of materiality repeats itself it creates a cube—the box of your thinking—of your material world of which we have spoken often. It must by its own nature imprison itself, so when you enter the cube/box of the physical world you easily 'imprison' yourself. Now you can go off and evaluate your world from outside the prison!

To describe this process another way, as the fourth creates manifestation it spins off its own new series of 'shapes' inherent in the original potential for manifestation. These we call 5, 6 and 7. The seventh, being the third aspect of this second or manifested triad, has the potential to give rise to its own string of manifested possibilities as it reflects, returns and yet 'journeys' out from its source.

The seventh in turn creates another square (eight) which in turn spawns another triad (9,10,11) and so on until the infinity of manifestation has run its course. Thus is the manifested universe infinite but bounded and by many views can this truth be known.

The potential of God can be said to be limitless but in this physical universe of which we speak, is bounded by the laws of manifestation, many of which have been presented in these books for your contemplation. The lesson is that with each tumbling forth a new reflection of divinity is seen and yet this is the illusion, for they are but prisms, triangular windows through which the human minds can view their source.

Each movement 'away' from God leads therefore to a window through which to view His all pervasive power and by which all His expressions—which are the organised substance we call the Mother or feminine aspect of God— receive His Light. Through the kaleidoscope of prisms must all manifested creation travel to find Father-Mother God is One, and the child and the parents One.

Do you see then how it is that relationship creates both the reality and illusion of man? Man's enemy is fear. It arises from your belief and investment that your world is real. We have said that your world is made of waves extending from God's thought. Since God is real, surely then these extensions must be real? But this confuses the thought with the thinker, the image with the mind capable of imagining any possibility. The void can be said to be the substance of the mind of God as your brain is the substance or inclination of your mind. It is the transit point through which your thinking is turned from energetic waves to the slower waves of solidification. These are analogies it is true but they hold for the purpose of your understanding.

What you fear is *no* thing—that what you thought was real is not, and in this indeed your fear has foundation for nothing of the cosmic physical planes is real, for it resides in God's imagining. Yet *God* is real and beneath all your fears is that there is no God, no heaven, no Earth, no hell, no angels . . . Why do you fear the Truth that the great imagining of God is not real? You have played in your movie so long you are afraid it will end and fear the moment when the lights come on again, and you find yourselves not the character you played but the actor, director and producer of the play. You fear that all will dissolve in illusion, yet it is the illusion you must dissolve before you can find yourself in Reality again.

It is a matter of identification. You can play for aeons happily in the planes of God's imagining but your happiness depends upon knowing it *is* play, and you never left your security of place as the essence of the thinker. But when you understand the relationship of God to His thinking you can safely play, aware of yourself on many planes, and fearing not, nor grieving any more for the illusion of these planes. For have I not just said that these are only one Reality of God's thinking and beyond imagination and comprehension now, are still greater universes?

When you can allow, without fear, *this* universe of planes to dissolve, to know it is illusion, but to Love it still, detached, unjudging, and with gratitude for the magnitude of God's thinking, you shall find yourself, not lost, not dead, not gone, but your true 'relationship' to God revealed.

We said that all forms, at bottom are spheres, coming into or losing their shape, but when seen from the perspective of the void, the sphere does not grow. It is already complete. In the Stillness and Darkness of God, everything that ever was or will be already *is*. It was at the beginning and has no ending. Beginning and ending are ideas arising from time and have no meaning in the ever present *now*.

From such understanding even the Spiritual Hierarchy is an illusion. It is only a hierarchy from a 'time/space' perception, from a 'point' along the wave. Even the progression of the planes is an illusion, the one becoming another in an endless parade of becoming. Without this movement it seems to you there is nothing, but that nothing *is* something. It is God.

God is a name you give to that which cannot be named, but it is sufficient for now that you call it so, and as long as you need words will you need to give 'God' a name. You can say that God is all there is, yet God is even more than this and such a mystery as what God is, is so great in its unfolding that here we have but glimpsed the first stages of its comprehension, and even the seven planes and the many 'heavens' are but way-stops to the greater heaven.

All that we have said is true, but in the grasping of this truth a greater Truth stands yet to be revealed to you. How quickly and gladly will you move, when the Truth we have outlined for you becomes not theory but the constant living consciousness of every moment for you. All the struggles of your world shall fall away and cease to be as in a dream whose reality has gone, on waking.

And as your tiny self is dropped and falls away, the planes of cosmic being will open up to you. What we have in these volumes described is how God 'creates' the cosmic planes upon which all the physical realities of those planes dwell. It is a neat and ordered plan, although it seems not so to those stuck in the chaotic confusion of the mind of man!

At every age the sages have described the unfolding of Creation for you in language made to strike a chord of understanding. But those descriptions are indeed just a stage of understanding. In the history of man there have been waves of understanding as each 'class' 'graduates' to the next level of knowing, and for a time, darkness seems to overtake the rest as they struggle on, leaderless, for the wise amongst them have moved on, beyond their reach it seems to the tiny minds of those they left behind. Then in slow learning the remainder must themselves move up and on, eventually to understand that those who left are still accessible, standing not 'above' but beside them in finer, more refined states of being, aware energetically of those in their surrounding planes, themselves reaching out for greater understanding, both poised and flying across the sacred miles of the journey. Now they have the freedom, as you too shall have quite soon, of travelling between a multitude of realms across God's many planes and residing simultaneously in His Stillness, to know all that is, in the Silence of God's creating Dark.

In that Darkness shall you find yourself as if lost in a vast ocean—the 'waters' of His void, and just as it seems there is nothing at all in God's ocean, you will know it contains all His dreams, and you shall turn as a fish turns to seek another prey, and dive inside the potential of that ocean to find yourself amidst the indigo where space is endless. But as it moves apart shall you find the stars, and what was void and dark explode in brilliant Light. Not in chaos does this Light explode, but in ordered unfoldment as the sound of God's breath sings His colours forth. And all the potential that lay in the void is turned inside out and the seven great waves are the rays on which you 'travel' forth.

You will learn that colour and sound are all there is to any 'thing,' but even colour and sound are but re-finements of a finer resonance, a finer knowing of the greater, closer to the source of everything.

All the cosmic beings, the gods and demi gods, myths, legends, angels, fairies, goblins and every such thing will be known to you, not in the distortion of the tiny egocentric view, but rightly as what they genuinely are—energies— intelligent and belonging just as you belong. Then you shall fear them not, nor worship them, but love and accept them as the 'greater' or the 'lesser' parts of God that they are. All understanding can be yours, from the geometry of the cosmic plan to the dancing magic of they who wield the rain or populate the world with flowers and trees. All aspects of God shall you have access to, from the lava core of Earth to those who live in the fiery heat of every star.

And every form on every plane can be known to you and if you tire of these almost infinite of games, then nameless God remains, and at the gate of greater knowing shall you find yourself, not now in human form but as a graduated being, joined, infused and One with your own ray, at home, melded and fused with all the other beings who shared that ray with you. So waste not a moment in petty sorrow or claim to fame as victim or hero, but rejoice in Life and place yourself at God's disposal.

Epilogue

To Self

Where is the journey I thought so long?
'Twas here and now has gone
And home no heaven in far off land
But here at either hand

And what I thought was 'up' or 'down'
Is really all around
Penetrating Earth and sky
And seeping through the ground

This life divides me not
From planes where angels dwell
And only my refusal
To know myself is 'hell'

For I AM an angel,
Each particle of me
And the Light of angel singing
Is there for me to see

God waits not on far off throne
And judges not my play
But Mother, Father, All in One,
Is subtle night and bright lit day

There is no 'Him,' nor 'It,' nor 'me'
For truly all is One
This energy divine is Life
And all worlds God—the Son.

Index

This World of Echoes —A Divine Guide to Being Human
is available as three separate eBooks.
Log in to your retailer of choice or check the eBook links via
either of the website addresses below where you will also find
more information about *This World of Echoes.*

www.jacquelynelane.com

or

www.worldofechoes.com

Email: info@worldofechoes.com